AS IS

some pencil

D0897080

LEOPARDI: POEMS AND PROSE

Leopardi

POEMS AND PROSE

EDITED BY ANGEL FLORES

Introduction by Sergio Pacifici

―――――

With the Italian Text of the Poems

INDIANA UNIVERSITY PRESS

Bloomington and London

Copyright © 1966 by Indiana University Press

All rights reserved

No part of this book may be reproduced or utilized in any form
or by any means, electronic or mechanical, including photocopy-
ing, recording, or by any information storage and retrieval sys-
tem, without permission in writing from the publisher.

Library of Congress catalog card number: 66-22450

Manufactured in the United States of America

ISBN 0-253-20094-6

2 3 4 5 6   80 79 78 77 76

CONTENTS

From *Operette Morali*

From *Pensieri*

INTRODUCTION

GIACOMO LEOPARDI: AN INTRODUCTION

Except to the specialist in foreign literatures, and to a small nucleus of sophisticated readers, the name of Giacomo Leopardi has remained largely ignored in this country, for reasons that are difficult to explain. Thus, in the engrossing story of the American "encounter" with Italy—an encounter that has reached a meaningful dimension only in the last decade—the publication of an anthology of the work of Italy's finest lyric poet ranks as a particularly important event. For a long time, in fact, professional critics have unanimously agreed that in modern times Italy has produced two writers of international stature: Alessandro Manzoni, author of *I Promessi Sposi*, one of the masterpieces of Western European fiction, and Giacomo Leopardi, whose *Canti* synthesize the spirit of his era and in some ways anticipate much of our own. Both artists, despite the diametrically opposite position they occupy in the cultural map of their country and for all the vast differences that mark their outlook and work, are pivotal, seminal figures in their literature. What they wrote had a profound, if often indirect, effect upon their contemporaries and the generations of writers who followed them. Indeed, without understanding their literary achievement, the quality of their vision, and the complexity of their poetics, it is well-nigh impossible to perceive with clarity the development of Italian fiction and poetry from their day to ours.

In the history of modern Italy it would indeed be difficult to find two writers who so unmistakenly epitomize, in the brilliant definition of Leonardo Olschki, "the polarity of the Italian spiritual heritage and of contemporary European trends of thought and action." Both men came from noble families; both possessed unusually sensitive, aristocratic minds. For all their widely diverse intellectual preparation and experiences, both were able to overcome the provincial patriotism and the cultural provincialism that characterize the work of many of their contemporaries. But here the similarities would end: for while Manzoni's views and attitudes toward the world are shaped by a Christian optimism and a Dantesque, unshakeable faith in God's Providence, Leopardi's outlook is the product of an agnostic—not to say atheist—mind, whose bleak pessimism is occasionally redeemed by the hope that mankind might some day discover the meaning and necessity of human solidarity to protect itself from the injustices of Nature.

Of the two, I predict that most of today's readers will find Leopardi more interesting, partly because what he had to say will seem more in tune with the mood of our civilization, and partly because he was always grappling with existential questions that have haunted mankind since time immemorial: Why do we exist? What is the purpose and reason of our all-too-brief stay in this world? Why do we suffer? Is happiness, whether achieved through love or work, possible to man or is it a mere illusion? Leopardi's search—as reflected in his work —lacks the tranquillity of Manzoni; unlike him, Leopardi never found any reassuring, satisfying answers in religion, and this places him closer to a generation which, disappointed by religion and science alike, torn by wars, revolutions, and social changes of great magnitude, must nevertheless continue its search for what it considers to be the truths of existence.

In recent years, Leopardi's originality as a prose writer and as a theorist of poetry (who anticipated the practice of several modern poets from Baudelaire and Mallarmé to Saba, Ungaretti, and Montale) has received ample attention and recognition. Critic, student of poetry, scholar, and exceedingly good prose writer that he was, it is primarily as a poet that we justly continue to value him. He was the creator, not only of some of the most perfect compositions produced in modern times, but also (in Italy at any rate) of a lyric deeply imbued with philosophical ideas, capable equally of treating themes that are as timeless as they are universal, and of instilling into the "reader's spirit such a noble sentiment that, for half an hour, it prevents him from entertaining any base thought or from committing any unworthy act." Thus Leopardi amply fulfilled his own conception of the true usefulness of Art. His is, finally, a poetic voice that even in its darkest and most disconsolate moments cherishes not what is ignoble in life, but what is magnanimous and worth preserving. Indeed, everything he wrote may be regarded as an eloquent document of how he strove, even after having realized "the wretchedness of men and the nullity of things," to find a valid reason to cling to life. And life, for him at any rate, could be measured only by man's lasting creativity.

Leopardi was born at Recanati, a small, "savage town" in the Marches region, near the Adriatic Sea, on June 28, 1798. His father, Count Monaldo, was an archconservative but a literate man, with a genuine love of books if not of unorthodox ideas; his mother, Countess Adelaide Antici, was an austere, forbidding woman whose main preoccupation seems to have been the preservation of a small family estate that had been all but squandered by her husband's inept management.

There are actually few details one needs to know in connection with Leopardi's life, for his existence was singularly devoid of the dash and color of such contemporaries of his as Lord Byron and Ugo Foscolo. He lived in his native town until the age of twenty-four, when he succeeded in winning parental permission to go to Rome. From 1822 onwards, he lived and worked (mostly as an editor) in Rome, Bologna, Milan, Florence, and Pisa. He returned to Recanati only three times, and then for brief periods, and spent the last two years of his life, afflicted by numerous illnesses, in Naples, aided and comforted by a patient and loyal friend, Antonio Ranieri.

In his intellectual development the most noteworthy aspect of Leopardi's early life was the isolation of his formative years, in combination with his impressively diversified education that included training in theology, archeology, rhetoric, astronomy, philosophy, and languages. At the age of sixteen he had mastered Latin, French, Greek, and Hebrew, and had gained a working knowledge of Spanish and German. By 1817, he had translated Horace's *Ars Poetica,* Moschus' *Idylls,* and the *War of Frogs and Mice,* and parts of the *Aeneid* and of the *Odyssey;* he had completed several original works, including two tragedies, a *History of Astronomy,* an *Essay on the Popular Errors of the Ancients,* and had even palmed off a "Hymn to Neptune" as an original Greek poem he claimed to have discovered during his research!

Such a list of achievements, which is far from complete, is bound to mislead the reader to conclude that by training and inclination Leopardi was a scholar, working in isolation to decipher and penetrate the mysteries of past civilizations. Nothing could be further from the truth. As in the case of other poets both before and after him—one thinks at once of Ezra Pound, T. S. Eliot, Marianne Moore, Robert Lowell, Ungaretti, and Quasimodo in our century—his extensive contact with works of classical antiquity was to serve many a function. First, it awakened in him a deep desire to be a poet in his own right. "I was not lacking in imagination," he wrote in his diary-notebook, *Zibaldone,* "but I never thought of myself as poet until I read the Greeks. . . . I did not lack enthusiasm, creative powers, and passions—but I did not believe myself to be eloquent until I had read Cicero." Second, as his friend Pietro Giordani perceptively observed, Leopardi "came to know the world of two thousand years ago long before he knew that of his own time; and what is more surprising, he learned what his own was, and how to value it." Finally, in translating the classics he had developed a first hand knowledge of, and feeling for the nuances, colors, rhythm, and value of words—a knowledge and feeling that were to serve him in good stead in his creative moments.

The year 1816 marked one of the important turning points of Leopardi's life, when first his literary taste, then his political ideas, changed drastically, At that time he underwent his "literary conversion," a transition from purely critical to creative activity. He began to draw closer to the French Romantics and discovered many of those poets of his native tradition whose work had been, up to that time, alien to his temperament: Dante, Petrarch (who had a lasting effect upon him), Tasso (with whose life he felt a special affinity), Alfieri, Metastasio, and Foscolo. At that time also, his political ideas, previously permeated by his father's conservatism, became more liberal. This emancipation was signalled by two *canzoni:* "To Italy" and "On Dante's Monument," both of which were composed in 1818 under the influence of Giordani, his first literary mentor, whose visit to Recanati that year had been one of the most memorable events of Leopardi's life.

By 1819, Leopardi had accomplished what most people would be content to achieve in a lifetime: he was a published scholar, highly esteemed by his colleagues, an editor whose services were increasingly in demand, and a poet whose lyrics (which had appeared in volume form the year before) had won immediate recognition. Yet his formative period, the "seven years of mad and desperate studies," had literally consumed him. Moreover, living in Recanati, a "horrible, detestable, execrated sepulchre, where the dead are happier than the living," a veritable "prison," had proven to be an experience that his temperament, which craved love, companionship, and understanding, found unbearable.

He came to despise violently the parochialism of his home town, the bigotry of its inhabitants, the sterile quality of Recanati's intellectual climate. Longing for communion with other men of letters, frustrated by his isolation, he became alienated from his own environment, by which he felt trapped. Strangely enough, it was in Recanati that Leopardi was to produce most of his finest work, and it was his abhorred native town that inspired some of his most tender lyrics. Meanwhile, the year 1819 proved to be yet another turning point in his own life.

Forced to idleness by a temporary blindness, he began brooding about his condition. "I began to feel my unhappiness," he recorded in his diary on July 1, 1820, "in a much gloomier manner. I began to abandon hope, and reflect deeply on things . . . to become a philosopher by profession (from the poet I was), to feel the necessary unhappiness of the world instead of knowing it." The construction of a philosophical system that would enable him to apprehend and systematize the essence of reality and of the human condition became an ambition, destined to remain unfulfilled.

An extensive examination of his philosophical notions, tempting as it is and instructive as it would be, is largely outside the scope of these brief introductory remarks. It might suffice to remark here that what Leopardi referred to as his philosophy, "*il mio sistema*," is less a logically constructed, carefully planned, and methodically developed study of reality and of human existence, than a series of sensitive statements that often contradict each other, written as they were in different "moods" and stages of his artistic development. Leopardi's philosophical trajectory is replete with reversals of previous positions. Thus, for example, he originally conceived the human condition in terms of a basic conflict between a vital and benign Nature and Reason, which erodes and ultimately destroys man by making him aware of the futility of his illusions. Soon enough, however, he began portraying Nature as a cruel, vicious, unforgiving "stepmother," insensitive to the plight of mankind and its fate, a declared "enemy of all human beings, of every kind and species." In the early part of his *Zibaldone* Leopardi stated that there were three fundamental ways to assess reality: that of the child and of the primitives, full of wonderment and expectations, preceding the disastrous confrontation with and apprehension of truth, happy but also short-lasting; that of the common man, who accepts the shabbiness, the mediocrity, of his existence, and succeeds in finding a modicum of happiness in his stance; and, finally, that of the sensitive person, who through reflection, study, and sensitivity perceives the void of life, and cannot help experiencing a metaphysical despair. A substantial share of Leopardi's lyrics bear the clear impact of the first and third positions just outlined; all constitute a haunting expression of a human revolt against the evil, the pain, and, above all, the suffering of life. In the last analysis, it is to his creative work that we must look to see how he managed to distill his philosophy into poetic images whose worth must perforce be determined by aesthetic rather than historical criteria. Furthermore, as George Santayana once shrewdly noted, "a poet has his worst moments when he tries to be a philosopher, or rather, when he succeeds in being one."

It is in his poems and many of the *Operette morali* that Leopardi corrected the negative, nihilistic views he had expressed in the *Zibaldone* and in the *Pensieri*. He allowed his feelings, deeply hurt by life, to settle in his memory, so that he could recapture them *after* the sting had been felt and had passed; he restudied them objectively, and gave them a new life by dramatizing them in dialogues woven out of the stuff of ancient myths, history, and literature. In his poems, too, he succeeded in seeing, and in making us see, in unforgettable scenes and vignettes, both the gelid indifference of Nature and her undeniable beauty. Occasionally, he achieved flashes of humor and gentle, mild expressions of hope. On the whole, his sentiments do not make for an optimistic vision; but they are indications of a certain serenity in the poet and the man. He could admit, and in a discreet sense reconcile, the coexistence of good and evil, happiness and misery, hope and disillusionment—even when he bitterly denounced the "infinite vanity of everything." As Nature reminds her interlocutor,

"Life in this universe is a perpetual cycle of production and destruction, so bound together that one is always counteracting the others, thus preserving the world which, if either ceased to operate, would likewise dissolve. Therefore if man did not suffer, the world itself might be destroyed."

Both in its best and worst moments, his poetic work mirrors the profound anguish and loneliness he experienced at every stage of his development as a human being and as an artist, the intense conflicts that had always torn a temperament refined and made hypersensitive by isolation and metaphysical despair of his existence. His life and work read like an absorbing study of contrasting forces—of hopes constantly dashed by disappointments, of loves yearned for but never attained, of fervent programs and total renunciations, of glories desired but never conferred. For a long time he had wanted to leave Recanati and escape an intolerable parental vigilance. When he finally succeeded, he was so revolted by the frivolity and intellectual corruption of the big cities that he longed to return to his native town. Similarly, whereas in his youth he had entertained "a great desire—perhaps an immodest and insolent one—for fame," he eventually discovered that fame, along with Glory, Patriotism, Virtue, and sensual Love, are but illusions shattered by the "wisdom" we acquire when we become truly adult. So it was with everything in his life—and so indeed it had to be: for our dreams, with which we nourish ourselves when we are children, are always larger and more perfect than reality; even when realized, they seldom bring us anything more than a feeling of dissatisfaction for we always look beyond for more than we have. The fruit of our pleasure is never as sweet as our anticipation of its savor, or as our memory of the moment when it was ours to enjoy: this is the theme of "Village Saturday," repeated, in yet another form in the *operetta* "Dialogue between an Almanac Peddler and a Passer-by." The good life is not the one we know, but the one we do not know. Isn't it the mystery of a future that has at least the possibility of bringing us the happiness we have not attained in the past that enables man to cling to life? "Illusions," Leopardi noted in 1820, "however weakened and unmasked by reason, still remain and form the chief part of our life"; and "the most solid pleasure in this life is the empty pleasure of illusion." In our century, such disparate playwrights as Luigi Pirandello and Edward Albee have echoed similar views. To escape the trap of ennui—which Leopardi defined as "the desire for happiness, left, so to speak, pure"—he must (like Columbus) engage in dangerous exploits that keep him continuously struggling for survival and thereby stave off despair.

If much of the conceptual world of our poet (as it has been briefly outlined in this introduction) has a familiar ring, it is because his thinking echoes the writings of a large number of authors, from Pascal to Locke and Condillac, from La Rochefoucauld, Voltaire, and Rousseau to Mme de Stäel, with whom Leopardi was intimately familiar. What matters for the student of poetry, however, is less the originality of Leopardi's notions than the manner in which he chose to give them life through concrete, limpid, almost palpable images. To achieve this, the poet sought to refashion a language that after the Renaissance had grown academic, insipid, affected, and eventually created out of it a personal vocabulary. The arduous and demanding process was to occupy him throughout his creative years, as the numerous drafts and hundreds of corrections to which he subjected his compositions eloquently attest. He shunned words that were too literary, preferring instead the unassuming, limited vocabulary of the ordinary man, for, as he so lucidly stated, "the last things that a man reaches who wishes to express the movement of his heart are simplicity and naturalness." He drew abundantly from the poetic idiom of Dante, Petrarch, Tasso, and Metastasio, frequently choosing archaic words because they lent a flavor of the ancient, and because, in his view, their exclusion from common usage had impoverished the Italian language. Whenever possible, he carefully selected words capable of bringing out the vague, indefinite, and indefinable elements of the feelings he wished to convey to his readers. It is this very quality of style that makes such a poem as "The Infinite" so richly suggestive and evocative.

His finished work demonstrates that his was the most appropriate language to express the private events that he succeeded in transforming into universal experiences beyond history and geography. The scenes, his landscapes, his everpresent moon, the birds, the songs, the people that live in his lyrics—farmers, artisans, shepherds, townsfolk—all have become truly an integral part of the sensibility of generations of Italian readers.

It is Leopardi the careful craftsman, the artist with a sensitive ear for the cadence of his diction, for the value, the weight and resonance of each word that he employed in his verses, the patient master of the *mot juste,* who has served as a constant reminder to generations of poets after him (from the "Decadents" to the Futurists, from the *Rondisti* to the Hermetics) of the seriousness of their "trade," of the obligation of every artist to enrich and rejuvenate the standards of his art and his society.

Ever since his death, in 1837, although he has remained, as the distinguished critic Carlo Bo reminds us, "an isolated figure," his presence has served to sustain, and frequently inspire many of the best poets Italy has produced in modern times— Saba, Ungaretti, Montale, and Quasimodo among them. But, beyond the brilliant example of his style and diction, which De Sanctis rightly found to be the secret of the poet's genius, there is something else of moment.

It was Leopardi himself who, unconsciously perhaps, supplied the best definition of the quality I am trying to define: "All works of genius," he wrote, "have this in common: even when they demonstrate and make us perceive the inevitable unhappiness of life, even when they express the most dreadful despair, they nevertheless comfort the noble soul that finds itself in a state of depression, disillusionment, nullity, boredom, and discouragement, or in the most bitter and deadening misfortunes. Such works rekindle our enthusiasm, and though they treat and represent nothing but death, give back [to us] that life that had been lost."

SERGIO PACIFICI

I

Canti

ALL'ITALIA

O patria mia, vedo le mura e gli archi
E le colonne e i simulacri e l'erme
Torri degli avi nostri,
Ma la gloria non vedo,
Non vedo il lauro e il ferro ond'eran carchi
I nostri padri antichi. Or fatta inerme,
Nuda la fronte e nudo il petto mostri.
Oimè quante ferite,
Che lividor, che sangue! oh qual ti veggio
Formosissima donna! Io chiedo al cielo
E al mondo: dite dite;
Chi la ridusse a tale? E questo è peggio,
Che di catene ha carche ambe le braccia;
Sì che sparte le chiome e senza velo
Siede in terra negletta e sconsolata,
Nascondendo la faccia
Tra le ginocchia, e piange.
Piangi, che ben hai donde, Italia mia,
Le genti a vincer nata
E nella fausta sorte e nella ria.

Se fosser gli occhi tuoi due fonti vive,
Mai non potrebbe il pianto
Adeguarsi al tuo danno ed allo scorno;
Che fosti donna, or sei povera ancella.
Chi di te parla o scrive,
Che, rimembrando il tuo passato vanto,
Non dica: già fu grande, or non è quella?
Perché, perché? dov'è la forza antica,
Dove l'armi e il valore e la costanza?
Chi ti discinse il brando?
Chi ti tradì? qual arte o qual fatica

TO ITALY

O my country, I see the walls and arches
The columns and altars, the statues
And towers our ancestors built.
I see no glory.
I see no laurels, no armor,
Safeguard of our forebears. Defenseless,
Your forehead bare,
Your breast uncovered,
You are wounded and bruised,
And bleeding!
Alas, that I should ever find you thus,
Most beautiful woman!
I ask heaven
And earth: "Tell me, tell me
Who has degraded her?" Even worse,
Her arms are bound in heavy chains,
Hair dishevelled, without a veil,
Forgotten and inconsolable, on the ground, she sits
And hides her face
Between her knees, and weeps.
Weep, my Italy, you have reason to weep
For a people born to conquer,
Now suffer a cruel destiny.

If your eyes were two spouting springs,
Never could they shed enough tears
To mourn your ruin, and the scorn you suffer.
A noblewoman once, now a wretched slave,
All who write or talk of you,
Recalling your proud past,
Say: "You were great once; no more—"
Why? Why? Where is your former strength?

O qual tanta possanza
Valse a spogliarti il manto e l'auree bende?
Come cadesti o quando
Da tanta altezza in così basso loco?
Nessun pugna per te? non ti difende
Nessun de' tuoi? L'armi, qua l'armi: io solo
Combatterò, procomberò sol io.
Dammi, o ciel, che sia foco
Agl'italici petti il sangue mio.

Dove sono i tuoi figli? Odo suon d'armi
E di carri e di voci e di timballi:
In estranie contrade
Pugnano i tuoi figliuoli.
Attendi, Italia, attendi. Io veggio, o parmi,
Un fluttuar di fanti e di cavalli,
E fumo e polve, e luccicar di spade
Come tra nebbia lampi.
Né ti conforti? e i tremebondi lumi
Piegar non soffri al dubitoso evento?
A che pugna in quei campi
L'itala gioventude? O numi, o numi:
Pugnan per altra terra itali acciari.
Oh misero colui che in guerra è spento,
Non per li patrii lidi e per la pia
Consorte e i figli cari,
Ma da nemici altrui
Per altra gente, e non può dir morendo:
Alma terra natia,
La vita che mi desti ecco ti rendo.

Oh venturose e care e benedette
L'antiche età, che a morte
Per la patria correan le genti a squadre;
E voi sempre onorate e gloriose,

Your weapons? Your valor? Your endurance?
Who stole your sword?
Who betrayed you? What kind of trickery,
What force robbed you
Of your mantle and your golden trophies?
When and how did you plummet
From such a great height?
Will no one fight for you, no one defend you,
Not one of your men? Weapons, give me weapons,
And I alone will fight, and fall alone.
O Heaven, grant me this:
May my blood enflame the hearts of all Italians!

Where are your sons? I hear the sound of weapons,
And wagons, drums and voices;
Your young men fight
In foreign lands.
Beware, Italy, beware! I seem to see
Riders and horses surging back and forth,
And smoke, and dust, and the glitter of swords,
Like lightning among clouds.
Helpless, you suffer
The sight of this terrible battle.
What do Italian youth fight for
In alien fields? Oh, Heavens, Heavens!
Italian swordsmen fight on foreign soil!
How desolate, to die in war
Not for their homeland,
Not for their faithful wife
And loving children.
Killed by enemies not their own,
Dying, they cannot say:
"Sacred land of my birth,
The life you gave me
I give back to you."

O tessaliche strette,
Dove la Persia e il fato assai men forte
Fu di poch'alme franche e generose!
Io credo che le piante e i sassi e l'onda
E le montagne vostre al passeggere
Con indistinta voce
Narrin siccome tutta quella sponda
Coprìr le invitte schiere
De' corpi ch'alla Grecia eran devoti.
Allor, vile e feroce,
Serse per l'Ellesponto si fuggia,
Fatto ludibrio agli ultimi nepoti;
E sul colle d'Antela, ove morendo
Si sottrasse da morte il santo stuolo,
Simonide salia,
Guardando l'etra e la marina e il suolo.

E di lacrime sparso ambe le guance,
E il petto ansante, e vacillante il piede,
Toglieasi in man la lira:
Beatissimi voi,
Ch'offriste il petto alle nemiche lance
Per amor di costei ch'al Sol vi diede;
Voi che la Grecia cole, e il mondo ammira.
Nell'armi e ne' perigli
Qual tanto amor le giovanette menti,
Qual nell'acerbo fato amor vi trasse?
Come sì lieta, o figli,
L'ora estrema vi parve, onde ridenti
Correste al passo lacrimoso e duro?
Parea ch'a danza e non a morte andasse
Ciascun de' vostri, o a splendido convito:
Ma v'attendea lo scuro
Tartaro, e l'onda morta;
Né le spose vi foro o i figli accanto

O for that cherished and blessed age!
In ancient times, men marched in phalanxes,
To die for their country.
And in the Thessalian pass,
Honored in history,
Men, few in number,
Stood against Persia, battling destiny.
The fields, the rocks, the mountains, the waves,
Quietly reveal to the passing stranger,
Or so I believe, how the whole shore
Was covered with valiant men
Who sacrificed their life to Greece.
Then savage Xerxes
Took flight down to the Hellespont,
Branded with dishonor forever.
And on the hill of Antella, where the blessed phalanx perished,
Simonides ascended, and looked at the air, the sea and sun,
And retrieved them from death.

Tears streaming down his face,
Trembling, his heart heavy,
He took hold of his lyre:
"O happy men,
You bared your breast to enemy lances
For love of life and freedom;
You were honored by Greece, admired by the world,
What devotion led these youths to fight and face danger?
What love dragged you to a bitter death?
O sons, what made your final hour
So happy and serene, as laughing you ran
Onto the field of sorrow,
As if each one were going
Not to his death, but to a dance or feast?
But what awaited you was Tartarus,

Quando su l'aspro lito
Senza baci moriste e senza pianto.

Ma non senza de' Persi orrida pena
Ed immortale angoscia.
Come lion di tori entro una mandra
Or salta a quello in tergo e sì gli scava
Con le zanne la schiena,
Or questo fianco addenta or quella coscia;
Tal fra le Perse torme infuriava
L'ira de' greci petti e la virtute.
Ve' cavalli supini e cavalieri;
Vedi intralciare ai vinti
La fuga i carri e le tende cadute,
E correr fra' primieri
Pallido e scapigliato esso tiranno;
Ve' come infusi e tinti
Del barbarico sangue i greci eroi,
Cagione ai Persi d'infinito affanno,
A poco a poco vinti dalle piaghe,
L'un sopra l'altro cade. Oh viva, oh viva:
Beatissimi voi
Mentre nel mondo si favelli o scriva.

Prima divelte, in mar precipitando,
Spente nell'imo strideran le stelle,
Che la memoria e il vostro
Amor trascorra o scemi.
La vostra tomba è un'ara; e qua mostrando
Verran le madri ai parvoli le belle
Orme del vostro sangue. Ecco io mi prostro,
O benedetti, al suolo,
E bacio questi sassi e queste zolle,
Che fien lodate e chiare eternamente
Dall'uno all'altro polo.

And a black wave of death.
Your wives were far away, your sons not at your side,
As you lay on the bitter shore.
You died. No one kissed you, no one wept.

"You inflicted great pain and endless anguish
On the Persians.
As a lion breaks into a herd,
And leaps on the back of many a victim,
And with his claws
Rips into flesh,
So the Greeks with wild male fury
Fell upon the Persians.
See the dead horses and riders.
See how the chariots in flight
And the tangle of tents enmesh the defeated.
The tyrant, pale and dishevelled,
Is one of the first to flee.
See how the Greek heroes
Bathed in barbarians' blood,
Terrify the Persians.
One by one they succumbed to their wounds,
One by one they fell dead.
Hail to your glory! You remain blessed,
As long as men shall speak and write.

"Stars will fall screaming
Into the deep sea
Before the memory of your devotion is lost.
Your grave is an altar
Where mothers will bring their children
To see where your blood flowed.
O blessed heroes,
Here I will kneel down,
And kiss the stony ground!

Deh foss'io pur con voi qui sotto, e molle
Fosse del sangue mio quest'alma terra.
Che se il fato è diverso, e non consente
Ch'io per la Grecia i moribondi lumi
Chiuda prostrato in guerra,
Così la vereconda
Fama del vostro vate appo i futuri
Possa, volendo i numi,
Tanto durar quanto la vostra duri.

BRUTO MINORE

Poi che divelta, nella tracia polve
Giacque ruina immensa
L'italica virtute, onde alle valli
D'Esperia verde, e al tiberino lido,
Il calpestio de' barbari cavalli
Prepara il fato, e dalle selve ignude
Cui l'Orso algida preme,
A spezzar le romane inclite mura
Chiama i gotici brandi;
Sudato, e molle di fraterno sangue,
Bruto per l'atra notte in erma sede,
Fermo già di morir, gl'inesorandi
Numi e l'averno accusa,
E di feroci note
Invan la sonnolenta aura percote.

Stolta virtù, le cave nebbie, i campi
Dell'inquiete larve

You will be honored forever,
To the ends of the earth.
O if I could be with you,
My blood soaked into the soil!
Though fate has not decreed
That I should fall in war
And die for Greece,
Your poet may, by the grace of the gods,
Record your deeds for the future,
And share the glory of your fame."

RUTH YORCK & KENWARD ELMSLIE

BRUTUS MINOR

Now that uprooted in the Thracian dust
Italic virtue lay
A massive ruin, whence, for the Tiber's shore
And green Hesperian vales, the fates prepare
The trampling hoofbeats of Barbarian horse
And from the barren forests of the North
Under the chillstruck Bear
Summon the Gothic arms to batter down
The storied walls of Rome,
Sweat-bathed and dripping with fraternal blood
In lonely seat beneath the shadowed night
Resolved on dying, Brutus challenges
The Gods inexorable
And with ferocious notes
Strikes vainly on the slumber-laden air.

"Insensate virtue, empty clouds and fields
Of troubled fantasies;

Son le tue scole, e ti si volge a tergo
Il pentimento. A voi, marmorei numi,
(Se numi avete in Flegetonte albergo
O su le nubi) a voi ludibrio e scherno
È la prole infelice
A cui templi chiedeste, e frodolenta
Legge al mortale insulta.
Dunque tanto i celesti odii commove
La terrena pietà? dunque degli empi
Siedi, Giove, a tutela? e quando esulta
Per l'aere il nembo, e quando
Il tuon rapido spingi,
Ne' giusti e pii la sacra fiamma stringi?

Preme il destino invitto e la ferrata
Necessità gl'infermi
Schiavi di morte: e se a cessar non vale
Gli oltraggi lor, de' necessarii danni
Si consola il plebeo. Men duro è il male
Che riparo non ha? dolor non sente
Chi di speranza è nudo?
Guerra mortale, eterna, o fato indegno,
Teco il prode guerreggia,
Di cedere inesperto; e la tiranna
Tua destra, allor che vincitrice il grava,
Indomito scollando si pompeggia,
Quando nell'alto lato
L'amaro ferro intride,
E maligno alle nere ombre sorride.

Spiace agli Dei chi violento irrompe
Nel Tartaro. Non fora
Tanto valor ne' molli eterni petti.
Forse i travagli nostri, e forse il cielo
I casi acerbi e gl'infelici affetti

Such are your schools and treading on your heels
Repentance comes. To you, O marble Gods
(Whether your dwelling be by Phlegethon
Or in the Heavens) mere sport and mockery
Is that unhappy race
From whom you ordered temples, and a false
Ethic affronts mankind.
So deeply then is stirred celestial hate
By piety of earth? So guardian of the wicked
Thou sittest, mighty Jove, and when the cloud
Splits in the air, and when
Thou hurlest thy swift bolt,
It is to blast the pious and the just?

"Unconquered Fate and iron necessity
Oppress the sickly slaves
Of death; the base man, impotent to check
The evils they inflict, resigns himself
To necessary ill. Is injury less harsh
That knows no remedy? Feels he not grief
Who is deprived of hope?
Nay, mortal, never-ending war, vile Fate,
With you the hero wages,
Untutored in submission, and shakes off
Your hand despotic when it weighs on him
In triumph, and assumes a haughty stance
As deep into his flank
He thrusts the bitter blade
And greets the darkness with sardonic smile.

"The Gods approve not him who violently
Thrusts into Tartarus;
Weakling immortal breasts have not such valor
It may be all our travails and harsh trials
And sad affections Heaven has disposed

Giocondo agli ozi suoi spettacol pose?
Non fra sciagure e colpe,
Ma libera ne' boschi e pura etade
Natura a noi prescrisse,
Reina un tempo e Diva. Or poi ch'a terra
Sparse i regni beati empio costume,
E il viver macro ad altre leggi addisse;
Quando gl'infausti giorni
Virile alma ricusa,
Riede natura, e il non suo dardo accusa?

Di colpa ignare e de' lor proprii danni
Le fortunate belve
Serena adduce al non previsto passo
La tarda età. Ma se spezzar la fronte
Ne' rudi tronchi, o da montano sasso
Dare al vento precipiti le membra,
Lor suadesse affanno;
Al misero desio nulla contesa
Legge arcana farebbe
O tenebroso ingegno. A voi, fra quante
Stirpi il cielo avvivò, soli fra tutte,
Figli di Prometeo, la vita increbbe;
A voi le morte ripe,
Se il fato ignavo pende,
Soli, o miseri, a voi Giove contende.

E tu dal mar cui nostro sangue irriga,
Candida luna, sorgi,
E l'inquieta notte e la funesta
All'ausonio valor campagna esplori.
Cognati petti il vincitor calpesta,
Fremono i poggi, dalle somme vette
Roma antica ruina;
Tu sì placida sei? Tu la nascente

As pleasing spectacles for idle hours.
Not amidst guilt and grief
But free and pure among the forests wild
Nature, our goddess-queen
Long since prescribed our lives. Now that such rule
Of bliss has been o'erthrown by evil use,
Subjecting our scant days to other laws,
Say, when a virile soul,
Disdains his ill-starred days
Shall Nature blame a weapon not her own?

"Witless of guilt and of their own distress
Dumb animals, content,
Are led serenely through long lasting age
To the unsuspected pass. But should their pain
Lead them to dash their heads on hardy trunks
Or yield their limbs from lofty mountain tops
Precipitate to the wind,
Such miserable caprice would find no let
In law mysterious
Or misty logic. Nay to you alone
Of all the breeds by Heaven granted life,
O children of Prometheus, life is drear,
Likewise to you alone
When abject Fate impends
The shores of death doth Jupiter deny.

"And thou, from out the sea fed by our blood
Arisest, pallid moon,
The troubled night exploring and the heath
Ill-omened for Ausonia's chivalry.
Lo, on his kinsman's breast the victor treads,
The shuddering hills resound and from their heights
Old Rome plunges to ruin—
So placid art thou still? Thou didst behold

Lavinia prole, e gli anni
Lieti vedesti, e i memorandi allori;
E tu su l'alpe l'immutato raggio
Tacita verserai quando ne' danni
Del servo italo nome,
Sotto barbaro piede
Rintronerà quella solinga sede.

Ecco tra nudi sassi o in verde ramo
E la fera e l'augello,
Del consueto obblio gravido il petto,
L'alta ruina ignora e le mutate
Sorti del mondo: e come prima il tetto
Rosseggerà del villanello industre,
Al mattutino canto
Quel desterà le valli, e per le balze
Quella l'inferma plebe
Agiterà delle minori belve.
Oh casi! oh gener vano! abbietta parte
Siam delle cose; e non le tinte glebe,
Non gli ululati spechi
Turbò nostra sciagura,
Né scolorò le stelle umana cura.

Non io d'Olimpo o di Cocito i sordi
Regi, o la terra indegna,
E non la notte moribondo appello;
Non te, dell'atra morte ultimo raggio,
Conscia futura età. Sdegnoso avello
Placàr singulti, ornàr parole e doni
Di vil caterva? In peggio
Precipitano i tempi; e mal s'affida
A putridi nepoti
L'onor d'egregie menti e la suprema
De' miseri vendetta. A me dintorno

Lavinia's brood a-borning,
The deathless laurels and the happy years,
And thou in silence wilt shed on the hills
Thy bright unchanging ray, when to the shame
Of servile Italy
That same abandoned site
Will echo footfalls of Barbarian tribes.

"Mark how, twixt barren stones, on verdant bough
Both bird and beast sleep on,
Wonted oblivion heavy on their breasts,
Ignoring the great fall and the reversed
Fortunes of men: no sooner shall the roof
Of the industrious peasant blush with dawn
Than with his morning song
One will arouse the vale, and o'er the slopes
The other harry hard
The weakling plebs of all the lesser beasts.
O chance and change! O fruitless race! A part
Abject of things are we, the blood-stained clods,
The battle-echoing caves
Are moved not by our fate
Nor does our human anguish dim the stars.

"To deaf Olympian or Stygian lords
I make no last appeal,
I die invoking neither Earth nor Night
Nor thee, last ray of darkling death, discreet
Posterity. Was e'er offended grave
Appeased by tears, assuaged by words or gifts
Of a base age? To worser days our times
Precipitate; ill were it to entrust
To putrid sons of sons
The honor of great minds and the supreme
Vengeance of souls undone. Let the dark bird

Le penne il bruno augello avido roti;
Prema la fera, e il nembo
Tratti l'ignota spoglia;
E l'aura il nome e la memoria accoglia.

ALLA PRIMAVERA
O DELLE FAVOLE ANTICHE

Perché i celesti danni
Ristori il sole, e perché l'aure inferme
Zefiro avvivi, onde fugata e sparta
Delle nubi la grave ombra s'avvalla;
Credano il petto inerme
Gli augelli al vento, e la diurna luce
Novo d'amor desio, nova speranza
Ne' penetrati boschi e fra le sciolte
Pruine induca alle commosse belve;
Forse alle stanche e nel dolor sepolte
Umane menti riede
La bella età, cui la sciagura e l'atra
Face del ver consunse
Innanzi tempo? Ottenebrati e spenti
Di febo i raggi al misero non sono
In sempiterno? ed anco,
Primavera odorata, inspiri e tenti
Questo gelido cor, questo ch'amara
Nel fior degli anni suoi vecchiezza impara?

Vivi tu, vivi, o santa
Natura? vivi e il dissueto orecchio
Della materna voce il suono accoglie?
Già di candide ninfe i rivi albergo,

Swoop on bloodthirsty wing;
Let beast oppress and tempests scatter wide
My unmarked bones, and may
The wind bear off my name and memory."

THOMAS G. BERGIN

TO SPRING

OR, ON THE ANCIENT FABLES

Though the warm sun reclaim
What winter had laid waste, the west wind lend
New breath of life to the dead air and banish
The clinging clouds of overshadowing skies;
Though venturing birds ascend
Defenselessly upon the winds, and morning,
Piercing the thickets, melting sheathing rime,
Waken expectancy and passion's bold
Dominion among the restless animals-
Does there at all the more within the cold,
Grief-buried souls of men
Revive one vestige of that lovely age
Too soon struck down by force
Of knowledge, by fevered grief? Are not the beams
Of Phoebus Apollo quenched, forever darkened
To man's abandoned race?
O odorous Spring, can you awaken gleams
Of life in a breast congealed, where hoarfrosts chill,
Disfigure my prime of life, its blossoms kill?

Are you alive, alive,
O sacred Nature? Alive? And can man's ear,
Unused to listen, hear the great mother's call?
Once the white naiads haunted banks of streams,

Placido albergo e specchio
Furo i liquidi fonti. Arcane danze
D'immortal piede i ruinosi gioghi
Scossero e l'ardue selve (oggi romito
Nido de' venti): e il pastorel ch'all'ombre
Meridiane incerte ed al fiorito
Margo adducea de' fiumi
Le sitibonde agnelle, arguto carme
Sonar d'agresti Pani
Udì lungo le ripe; e tremar l'onda
Vide, e stupì, che non palese al guardo
La faretrata Diva
Scendea ne' caldi flutti, e dall'immonda
Polve tergea della sanguigna caccia
Il niveo lato e le verginee braccia.

Vissero i fiori e l'erbe,
Vissero i boschi un dì. Conscie le molli
Aure, le nubi e la titania lampa
Fur dell'umana gente, allor che ignuda
Te per le piagge e i colli,
Ciprigna luce, alla deserta notte
Con gli occhi intenti il viator seguendo,
Te compagna alla via, te de' mortali
Pensosa immaginò. Che se gl'impuri
Cittadini consorzi e le fatali
Ire fuggendo e l'onte,
Gl'ispidi tronchi al petto altri nell'ime
Selve remoto accolse,
Viva fiamma agitar l'esangui vene,
Spirar le foglie, e palpitar segreta
Nel doloroso amplesso
Dafne o la mesta Filli, o di Climene
Pianger credé la sconsolata prole
Quel che sommerse in Eridano il sole.

Would into mirrors peer
Of lucid springs. Immortal feet once trod
Their secret dances, troubling the mountain-tops
And pathless woods (where desolate winds have made
Their dwellings since); the shepherd at still noon
Drove thirsting flocks within the tremulous shade
By flower-bordered brooks
And heard along the banks shrill songs arise
Of rustic Pans, or looked
Marveling on the water's agitation—
Where, though unseen, the arrow-quivered goddess
Descended the warm waves
After the bloody hunt, in satiation,
To cleanse from arms and sides, her virgin grace,
Defiling crimson stains and dust of the chase.

Alive were grass and flowers,
Alive the forests then. The breeze light,
The clouds, and Titan's lamp, the sun,
Knew men their kindred; then, O Cyprian star,
The traveler by night,
Alone, would fix his gaze on your naked beauty
Moving above the shores and hills, take you
As comrade of his journeying, his guide,
Imagining you man's friend. Another, leaving
Unnatural intercourse of towns, allied
To fatal strife and shame,
In woodland depths embraced the rough tree-trunks
And thought he felt life's fire
Course in the bloodless veins when every leaf
Trembled and seemed to breathe, as though he held
Daphne in sad embrace
There hidden within, or Phyllis in her grief,
Or Clymene's daughter, she who mourned for one
Cast in Eridanus by the mighty sun.

Né dell'umano affanno,
Rigide balze, i luttuosi accenti
Voi negletti ferìr mentre le vostre
Paurose latebre Eco solinga,
Non vano error de' venti,
Ma di ninfa abitò misero spirto,
Cui grave amor, cui duro fato escluse
Delle tenere membra. Ella per grotte,
Per nudi scogli e desolati alberghi,
Le non ignote ambasce e l'alte e rotte
Nostre querele al curvo
Etra insegnava. E te d'umani eventi
Disse la fama esperto,
Musico augel che tra chiomato bosco
Or vieni il rinascente anno cantando,
E lamentar nell'alto
Ozio de' campi, all'aer muto e fosco,
Antichi danni e scellerato scorno,
E d'ira e di pietà pallido il giorno.

Ma non cognato al nostro
Il gener tuo; quelle tue varie note
Dolor non forma, e te di colpa ignudo,
Men caro assai la bruna valle asconde.
Ahi, ahi, poscia che vote
Son le stanze d'Olimpo, e cieco il tuono
Per l'atre nubi e le montagne errando,
Gl'iniqui petti e gl'innocenti a paro
In freddo orror dissolve; e poi ch'estrano
Il suol nativo, e di sua prole ignaro
Le meste anime educa;
Tu le cure infelici e i fati indegni
Tu de' mortali ascolta,
Vaga natura, e la favilla antica
Rendi allo spirto mio; se tu pur vivi,

Nor, flinty cliffs, on you
Did voices of human sorrow strike unheard
When Echo, companionless, inhabited
Your awesome chasms and caverns; she was then
No quaint illusion stirred
By errant winds, the grieving ghost of a nymph
By unrequited love and fate cast out
From lovely limbs. From caves, from rocky shelves
And waste abodes, acquainted with sorrow, she
Repeated broken tones, the accents themselves
Of human woe to the skies
That arched above. And fame reported then,
Most musical nightingale,
With human deeds conversant (in leafy shades
Now ushering in the Spring reborn), how you
Lamented, as twilight came
On meadows stilled and on receding glades,
The ancient tragedy, vengeance, appeaseless blame
Of a day of wrath and anguish darkened with shame.

Your race is now no kindred
To ours; your varied notes express no woe
Like ours, and freed of guilt but less beloved
You sing in the valley mantled deep in darkness.
Alas, alas, we know
Olympus' dwellings empty; blinded thunder
Aimlessly wanders the black clouds and cliffs,
Dissolves in stricken fearfulness at once
Guilty and guiltless hearts; our native earth,
A mother indifferent, nurtures her sons
In alienation and sadness.
Fair Nature, yet on such unworthy doom,
Our mortal plight, take pity;
Rekindle the ancient flame within my heart—
If you indeed be living, if in heaven,

E se de' nostri affanni
Cosa veruna in ciel, se nell'aprica
Terra s'alberga o nell'equoreo seno,
Pietosa no, ma spettatrice almeno.

ULTIMO CANTO DI SAFFO

Placida notte, e verecondo raggio
Della cadente luna; e tu che spunti
Fra la tacita selva in su la rupe,
Nunzio del giorno; oh dilettose e care
Mentre ignote mi fur l'erinni e il fato,
Sembianze agli occhi miei; già non arride
Spettacol molle ai disperati affetti.
Noi l'insueto allor gaudio ravviva
Quando per l'etra liquido si volve
E per li campi trepidanti il flutto
Polveroso de' Noti, e quando il carro,
Grave carro di Giove a noi sul capo,
Tonando, il tenebroso aere divide.
Noi per le balze e le profonde valli
Natar giova tra' nembi, e noi la vasta
Fuga de' greggi sbigottiti, o d'alto
Fiume alla dubbia sponda
Il suono e la vittrice ira dell'onda.

Bello il tuo manto, o divo cielo, e bella
Sei tu, rorida terra. Ahi di cotesta
Infinita beltà parte nessuna
Alla misera Saffo i numi e l'empia
Sorte non fenno. A' tuoi superbi regni

On sunlit earth or ocean,
Something has being, dwelling not apart,
Which though it pity not, hears us and sees,
Though but spectator of our agonies.

DWIGHT DURLING

SAPPHO'S LAST SONG

Oh serene night, and you, shy beams
Of the waning moon, and you that peep
From the silent trees above the cliff,
Herald of the day: how dear and pleasing
Were your faces to my eyes, as long as
Fate and Furies were unknown to me;
But now such gentle sights no longer please
Those with hopeless passions; for us
Unwonted joy can only live again
When through the limpid ether and over
Trembling fields swirls the dusty
Surge of the South Wind, and the chariot,
The ponderous chariot of Jove, thundering
Above our heads, cleaves the tenebrous air.
To plunge into the storm above the cliffs
And deepest valleys is fitting sport for us;
For us the vast flight of terrified flocks,
And from the river's depth to the treacherous shore
The victorious fury of the waters' roar.

Fair is your mantle, heavenly sky, and fair
Are you, oh dewy earth. Alas, no share
Of all this infinite beauty was allotted
To unhappy Sappho by the gods and
Unkind fate. In your magnificent kingdom,

Vile, o natura, e grave ospite addetta,
E dispregiata amante, alle vezzose
Tue forme il core e le pupille invano
Supplichevole intendo. A me non ride
L'aprico margo, e dall'eterea porta
Il mattutino albor; me non il canto
De' colorati augelli, e non de' faggi
Il murmure saluta: e dove all'ombra
Degl'inchinati salici dispiega
Candido rivo il puro seno, al mio
Lubrico piè le flessuose linfe
Disdegnando sottragge,
E preme in fuga l'odorate spiagge.

Qual fallo mai, qual sì nefando eccesso
Macchiommi anzi il natale, onde sì torvo
Il ciel mi fosse e di fortuna il volto?
In che peccai bambina, allor che ignara
Di misfatto è la vita, onde poi scemo
Di giovanezza, e disfiorato, al fuso
Dell' indomita Parca si volvesse
 Il ferrigno mio stame? Incaute voci
Spande il tuo labbro: i destinati eventi
Move arcano consiglio. Arcano è tutto,
Fuor che il nostro dolor. Negletta prole
Nascemmo al pianto, e la ragione in grembo
De' celesti si posa. Oh cure, oh speme
De' più verd'anni! Alle sembianze il Padre,
Alle amene sembianze eterno regno
Diè nelle genti; e per virili imprese,
Per dotta lira o canto,
Virtù non luce in disadorno ammanto.

Morremo. Il velo indegno a terra sparto,
Rifuggirà l'ignudo animo a Dite,

Nature, I have become a dull and worthless
Guest, a despised lover; to your graceful
Forms I direct in vain my heart and eyes
In supplication. The sunny bank,
And the early dawn at heaven's gate
Smile not on me; neither the song
Of painted birds, nor the murmur
Of beech trees give me greeting; and where
In weeping willows' shade, a pure stream
Widens into a limpid pool, from my
Slippery foot the sinuous water
Disdainfully withdraws,
And presses in its flight the fragrant shores.

What crime was it, what abominable excess
Marked me before my birth, that heaven
And the face of Fortune frowned on me?
How sinned I as a child, when I did not know
That life is made of wrongs, that,
Bereft of youth and beauty, my harsh grey
Thread was spun on the spindle by Fate
Implacable? Imprudent words
Flow from your mouth; destiny's acts
Revolve on a hidden scheme. All is hidden,
Except our suffering. We are neglected offspring,
Born to weeping, and the reason for it
Remains in the lap of the gods. Oh the cares
And hopes of greener years! To appearances,
To fine appearances the Father gave
Eternal power over men: however great
The work, or skilled the song and lyric verse
Virtue does not shine in ugly dress.

I die. Its unworthy cloak scattered to the earth,
My naked soul will take refuge with Dis,

E il crudo fallo emenderà del cieco
Dispensator de'casi. E tu cui lungo
Amore indarno, e lunga fede, e vano
D'implacato desio furor mi strinse,
Vivi felice, se felice in terra
Visse nato mortal. Me non asperse
Del soave licor del doglio avaro
Giove, poi che perìr gl'inganni e il sogno
Della mia fanciullezza. Ogni più lieto
Giorno di nostra età primo s'invola.
Sottentra il morbo, e la vecchiezza, e l'ombra
Della gelida morte. Ecco di tante
Sperate palme e dilettosi errori,
Il Tartaro m'avanza; e il prode ingegno
Han la tenaria Diva,
E l'atra notte, e la silente riva.

IL PRIMO AMORE

Tornami a mente il dì che la battaglia
D'amor sentii la prima volta, e dissi:
Oimè, se quest'è amor, com'ei travaglia!

Che gli occhi al suol tuttora intenti e fissi,
Io mirava colei ch'a questo core
Primiera il varco ed innocente aprissi.

Ahi come mal mi governasti, amore!
Perché seco dovea sì dolce affetto
Recar tanto desio, tanto dolore?

E non sereno, e non intero e schietto,
Anzi pien di travaglio e di lamento
Al cor mi discendea tanto diletto?

And make amends for the cruel error of chance's
Blind dispenser. And you, for whose sake
I am possessed by long and fruitless love,
By lasting faith and the futile fury of
Unslaked desire, be happy—if happy
Any mortal born may live on earth.
Jove's miserly hand did not sprinkle
Me with benign liquor from his cask,
For the illusions and the dream of childhood
Years have perished. All the joyful days
Of our allotted time do vanish first,
Sickness and old age come after, then the shade
Of icy death. And now, of all those
Longed-for glories and sweet illusions only
Tartarus remains. Brave genius is
Thrall to the dark Goddess evermore,
To black night and the silent shore.

MURIEL KITTEL

FIRST LOVE

I recall the day when first
I fought the battle of love, I said,
—Alas, if this is love, I grieve!—
Eyes downcast, transfixed,
I marvelled how my innocent heart
ventured into new realms.
Ah, how badly you ruled me, love!
Why should sweet emotion
lead to such longing, and so much pain?
Divided, thwarted, and never serene,
filled with laments and despair,
still my heart drowned in delight.

Dimmi, tenero core, or che spavento,
Che angoscia era la tua fra quel pensiero
Presso al qual t'era noia ogni contento?

Quel pensier che nel dì, che lusinghiero
Ti si offeriva nella notte, quando
Tutto queto parea nell'emisfero:

Tu inquieto, e felice e miserando,
M'affaticavi in su le piume il fianco,
Ad ogni or fortemente palpitando.

E dove io tristo ed affannato e stanco
Gli occhi al sonno chiudea, come per febre
Rotto e deliro il sonno venia manco.

Oh come viva in mezzo alle tenebre
Sorgea la dolce imago, e gli occhi chiusi
La contemplavan sotto alle palpebre!

Oh come soavissimi diffusi
Moti per l'ossa mi serpeano, oh come
Mille nell'alma instabili, confusi

Pensieri si volgean! qual tra le chiome
D'antica selva zefiro scorrendo,
Un lungo, incerto mormorar ne prome.

E mentre io taccio, e mentre io non contendo,
Che dicevi o mio cor, che si partia
Quella per che penando ivi e battendo?

Il cuocer non più tosto io mi sentia
Della vampa d'amor, che il venticello
Che l'aleggiava, volossene via.

Senza sonno io giacea sul dì novello,
E i destrier che dovean farmi deserto,
Battean la zampa sotto al patrio ostello.

Tell me of your anguish, loving heart,
your terror at the thought
each contentment turns to weary irritation.
All day long, that thought persisted,
and at night, enticed by desire,
—when the world around seemed quiet—
you were restless, both happy and wretched.
I tossed and turned, and tired my bed,
and never stopped trembling.
Sad and afraid and spent,
I closed my eyes;
feverish phantasies kept me from sleep.
How clearly out of the dark
her tender image appeared; eyes sealed,
I contemplated her on my closed lids.
How subtly diffuse were the emotions
that snaked through my being!
A thousand confused thoughts
encircled my uncertain soul, like a light wind
ruffles hanging vines in an ancient forest,
whispering without end.
And while I remained silent, and failed to act,
why did you not speak out, my heart,
for she was going away, she who made you suffer and grieve.
I'd rather be seared
by the blaze of love
than be saved by the breeze that bears it away.
I lay sleepless at dawn,
while the horses, soon to leave me behind, abandoned,
stomped their hoofs in front of her house.
Fearful and silent and wary,
in the dark I leaned over the balcony,
eyes and ears now wide open,
hoping to hear her voice,
in case her lips uttered a parting word.

Ed io timido e cheto ed inesperto,
Ver lo balcone al buio protendea
L'orecchio avido e l'occhio indarno aperto,

La voce ad ascoltar, se ne dovea
Di quelle labbra uscir, ch'ultima fosse;
La voce, ch'altro il cielo, ahi, mi togliea.

Quante volte plebea voce percosse
Il dubitoso orecchio, e un gel mi prese,
E il core in forse a palpitar si mosse!

E poi che finalmente mi discese
La cara voce al core, e dé cavai
E delle rote il romorìo s'intese;

Orbo rimaso allor, mi rannicchiai
Palpitando nel letto e, chiusi gli occhi,
Strinsi il cor con la mano, e sospirai.

Poscia traendo i tremuli ginocchi
Stupidamente per la muta stanza,
Ch'altro sarà, dicea, che il cor mi tocchi?

Amarissima allor la ricordanza
Locommisi nel petto, e mi serrava
Ad ogni voce il core, a ogni sembianza.

E lunga doglia il sen mi ricercava,
Com'è quando a distesa Olimpo piove
Malinconicamente e i campi lava.

Ned io ti conoscea, garzon di nove
E nove Soli, in questo a pianger nato
Quando facevi, amor, le prime prove;

Quando in ispregio ogni piacer, né grato
M'era degli astri il riso, o dell'aurora
Queta il silenzio, o il verdeggiar del prato.

Ah, what else under the sun could rob me of so much?
Then vulgar voices jabbed at
my vigilant ears. I shivered,
and my troubled heart throbbed wildly.
At last my love's voice
reached my heart, only to be drowned
by the sound of wheels and horses' hoofs.
I remained alone. Huddling in bed,
trembling I pressed
my hand to my heart, and sighed.
Then I paced back and forth
in the silent room,
—What else—I said—can ever touch my heart?—
Bitter memories weighed on my chest
whenever a voice, a face,
reminded me of her.
I felt deluged by endless sorrow,
as if a distant heaven drenched
the fields with melancholy rain.
I barely knew you,
when you first encountered love,
youth of nine and nine summers, born to the quest for tears.
Despising all pleasure,
you gave no welcome to the smiling stars,
the silent dawn, the green grass.
The lustre of love lay mute
in my impassioned breast,
haven for love's beauty.
I still pursued my usual studies—
how pointless they seemed
compared to imagined desires!
O, how could I be so changeable!
Hurled from one love to another,
true—all life is pointless.
Only the inner dialogue of my heart

Anche di gloria amor taceami allora
Nel petto, cui scaldar tanto solea,
Che di beltade amor vi fea dimora.

Né gli occhi ai noti studi to rivolgea,
E quelli m'apparian vani per cui
Vano ogni altro desir creduto avea.

Deh come mai da me sì vario fui,
E tanto amor mi tolse un altro amore?
Deh quanto, in verità, vani siam nui!

Solo il mio cor piaceami, e col mio core
In un perenne ragionar sepolto,
Alla guardia seder del mio dolore.

E l'occhio a terra chino o in se raccolto,
Di riscontrarsi fuggitivo e vago
Né in leggiadro soffria né in turpe volto:

Che la illibata, la candida imago
Turbare egli temea pinta nel seno,
Come all'aure si turba onda di lago.

E quel di non aver goduto appieno
Pentimento, che l'anima ci grava,
E il piacer che passò cangia in veleno,

Per li fuggiti dì mi stimolava
Tuttora il sen: che la vergogna il duro
Suo morso in questo cor già non oprava.

Al cielo, a voi, gentili anime, io giuro
Che voglia non m'entrò bassa nel petto,
Ch'arsi di foco intaminato e puro.

Vive quel foco ancor, vive l'affetto,
Spira nel pensier mio la bella imago,
Da cui, se non celeste, altro diletto

Giammai non ebbi, e sol di lei m'appago.

gave me pleasure,
guarded me from grief.
Eyes downcast, self absorbed,
for a fleeting moment, I saw
I was prey to folly, vulnerable to evil.
I was afraid to stir up
the innocent image engraved in my heart
much as waves at dawn stir up a lake.
Yet, regret tormented my soul
for not having tasted delight:
pleasures denied turn to poison.
As the days flew by, I became aware
my heart no longer felt
the sharp bite of shame.
O, I swear to heaven, to you, tender spirits—
I shall keep my inner fire pure,
and never submit to dark desires.
This fire is alive, my love is still alive,
alive, her beautiful image moves through my thoughts,
and there I taste delights, heaven-sent.
With her alone, I am content.

KENWARD ELMSLIE & RUTH YORCK

IL PASSERO SOLITARIO

D'in su la vetta della torre antica,
Passero solitario, alla campagna
Cantando vai finché non more il giorno;
Ed erra l'armonia per questa valle.
Primavera dintorno
Brilla nell'aria, e per li campi esulta,
Sì ch'a mirarla intenerisce il core.
Odi greggi belar, muggire armenti;
Gli altri augelli contenti, a gara insieme
Per lo libero ciel fan mille giri,
Pur festeggiando il lor tempo migliore:
Tu pensoso in disparte il tutto miri;
Non compagni, non voli,
Non ti cal d'allegria, schivi gli spassi;
Canti, e così trapassi
Dell'anno e di tua vita il più bel fiore.

Oimè, quanto somiglia
Al tuo costume il mio! Sollazzo e riso,
Della novella età dolce famiglia,
E te german di giovinezza, amore,
Sospiro acerbo de' provetti giorni,
Non curo, io non so come; anzi da loro
Quasi fuggo lontano;
Quasi romito, e strano
Al mio loco natio,
Passo del viver mio la primavera.
Questo giorno ch'omai cede alla sera,
Festeggiar si costuma al nostro borgo.
Odi per lo sereno un suon di squilla,
Odi spesso un tonar di ferree canne,
Che rimbomba lontan di villa in villa.

THE SOLITARY SPARROW

From the very top of this ancient tower,
Oh solitary sparrow, you still sing on
To the countryside as long as daylight lasts;
And through the valley drifts your melody.
All around you, Spring
Gleams in the air and triumphs in the fields,
Melting the hearts of those who see it.
Hear the bleating flocks, the lowing herds!
The other birds, in happy rivalry,
Wheel in the clear sky a myriad times,
Rejoicing in their favorite season;
While you, pensive, watch it all apart;
With no flights, no companions,
You do not care for joy, and shun all sport;
But singing, you wear out
The year's finest flower and your life's.

Alas, how similar
My habits are to yours! Pleasure and laughter,
Sweet retinue of our early years,
And love, inseparable from youth
And old age's bitter sigh,
I do not care for, I know not why; rather
I seem to flee from them;
And like a hermit, and a stranger
To my native place,
I spend the Springtime of my life.
This day, already giving way to evening,
Our town is used to keep a holiday.
Hear the sound of bells through the quiet air,
And the frequent thunder of gunfire
Reverberating afar from village to village.

Tutta vestita a festa
La gioventù del loco
Lascia le case, e per le vie si spande;
E mira ed è mirata, e in cor s'allegra.
Io solitario in questa
Rimota parte alla campagna uscendo,
Ogni diletto e gioco
Indugio in altro tempo: e intanto il guardo
Steso nell'aria aprica
Mi fere il Sol che tra lontani monti,
Dopo il giorno sereno,
Cadendo si dilegua, e par che dica
Che la beata gioventù vien meno.

Tu, solingo augellin, venuto a sera
Del viver che daranno a te le stelle,
Certo del tuo costume
Non ti dorrai; che di natura è frutto
Ogni vostra vaghezza.
A me, se di vecchiezza
La detestata soglia
Evitar non impetro,
Quando muti questi occhi all'altrui core,
E lor fia voto il mondo, e il dì futuro
Del dì presente più noioso e tetro,
Che parrà di tal voglia?
Che di quest'anni miei? che di me stesso?
Ahi pentirommi, e spesso,
Ma sconsolato, volgerommi indietro.

All in holiday clothes,
The young people of the place
Leave their homes and pour into the streets,
To see and to be seen, with gladness in their hearts.
But I, going out alone
To this remote part of the country,
Put off for another time
All sport and pleasure: meanwhile my gaze,
Wandering through the luminous air,
Is struck by the sun that, beyond the distant hills,
The calm day over,
Sets and vanishes, and by this tells me
That the blessed time of youth does fade away.

Oh lonely bird, when you reach the evening
Of the life the stars have given you,
You will surely not lament
Your way of life; for all your longings
Are but the fruit of nature.
For myself, if it be not granted
That I escape the hated
Threshold of old age,
When these eyes no longer speak to other hearts,
And the world to them is empty, and the future
More wearisome and dismal than the present,
How shall such wishes seem?
And these my present years, and I myself?
Alas, I shall repent, and often
Shall look back, and not be comforted.

MURIEL KITTEL

L'INFINITO

Sempre caro mi fu quest'ermo colle,
E questa siepe, che da tanta parte
Dell'ultimo orizzonte il guardo esclude.
Ma sedendo e mirando, interminati
Spazi di là da quella, e sovrumani
Silenzi, e profondissima quiete
Io nel pensier mi fingo; ove per poco
Il cor non si spaura. E come il vento
Odo stormir tra queste piante, io quello
Infinito silenzio a questa voce
Vo comparando: e mi sovvien l'eterno,
E le morte stagioni, e la presente
E viva, e il suon di lei. Così tra questa
Immensità s'annega il pensier mio:
E il naufragar m'è dolce in questo mare.

LA SERA DEL DI' DI FESTA

Dolce e chiara è la notte e senza vento,
E queta sovra i tetti e in mezzo agli orti
Posa la luna, e di lontan rivela
Serena ogni montagna. O donna mia,
Già tace ogni sentiero, e pei balconi
Rara traluce la notturna lampa:
Tu dormi, che t'accolse agevol sonno
Nelle tue chete stanze; e non ti morde
Cura nessuna; e già non sai né pensi
Quanta piaga m'apristi in mezzo al petto.
Tu dormi: io questo ciel, che sì benigno

THE INFINITE

This hidden knoll has been always dear to me,
And this shrubbery, that keeps obscure
So much of the ultimate horizon.
But sitting now and gazing, illimitable
Spaces yonder, and superhuman
Silences, and profoundest quiet
Come to mind; where still the heart
Knows scarcely fear. And listening to the wind
Rustling in this greenery, to
That infinite silence I compare
This voice: and I ponder the eternal,
And the dead seasons, and the present
And living, and its sound. Thus in this immensity
My meditations drown:
And it is sweet to lose myself in this sea.

KATE FLORES

HOLIDAY EVENING

The night is windless—windlessly soft and clear;
The moon pauses tranquilly on the rooftops,
Hovers by the orchards, lights each far-off mountain
In a picture of calm. Already, O my dearest,
The walks have all gone silent, and the darkness
Gathers about the winking balconies
Where a few lamps appear: you are asleep,
Folded in natural rest in your still rooms;
No cares assail you: and least of all the knowledge
Or guess that you have pierced me to the heart.
You are asleep: I face this sky, which seems

Appare in vista, a salutar m'affaccio,
E l'antica natura onnipossente,
Che mi fece all'affanno. A te la speme
Nego, mi disse, anche la speme; e d'altro
Non brillin gli occhi tuoi se non di pianto.
Questo dì fu solenne: or da' trastulli
Prendi riposo; e forse ti rimembra
In sogno a quanti oggi piacesti, e quanti
Piacquero a te: non io, non già ch'io speri,
Al pensier ti ricorro. Intanto io chieggo
Quanto a viver mi resti, e qui per terra
Mi getto, e grido, e fremo. Oh giorni orrendi
In così verde etate! Ahi, per la via
Odo non lunge il solitario canto
Dell'artigian, che riede a tarda notte,
Dopo i sollazzi, al suo povero ostello;
E fieramente mi si stringe il core,
A pensar come tutto al mondo passa,
E quasi orma non lascia. Ecco è fuggito
Il dì festivo, ed al festivo il giorno
Volgar succede, e se ne porta il tempo
Ogni umano accidente. Or dov'è il suono
Di que' popoli antichi? or dov'è il grido
De' nostri avi famosi, e il grande impero
Di quella Roma, e l'armi, e il fragorio
Che n'andò per la terra e l'oceano?
Tutto è pace e silenzio, e tutto posa
Il mondo, e più di lor non si ragiona.
Nella mia prima età, quando s'aspetta
Bramosamente il dì festivo, or poscia
Ch'egli era spento, io doloroso, in veglia,
Premea le piume; ed alla tarda notte
Un canto che s'udia per li sentieri
Lontanando morire a poco a poco,
Già similmente mi stringeva il core.

A blessing to men's sight, and I salute it,
And salute nature, that old omnipotence
Which shaped me for affliction. (Hope? said nature:
Hope I deny you; as for a shining eye—
Only the tears you shed will shine in yours.)
This day was a holiday: but all its amusements
You have ended with sleep, remembering perhaps
In your dreams how many took to you today,
How many you took to: it is not my name
(I dare not hope) that comes to your mind. So here
I ask what life I can look for, and on this ground
I throw myself; shudder; call out. Such days of horror
In years of youth! And oh, when my ear catches,
Quite near, the workman's late and lonely song
Along the road at night, as he goes home
From pleasures of the day to his poor retreat:
How desperately my heart is seized by thoughts
Of everything earthly slipping through as if
It left no track to trace! Here is this day,
This holiday, that has fled, hungrily followed
By common and unfestive days; time comes
Hurrying every human act into the wings.
Where today is the clamor of ancient throats?
Where today are our great forefathers crying,
And the vast power and arms and roar of Rome
That covered land and sea? There is nothing now
But peace and silence; the world rests its case,
Our passions are not roused by them, they have gone.
When I was very young, and holidays
Were ardently looked forward to, the great day
Came and went, and left me wretched, wakeful,
Pressing my pillow; and at the dead of night
A voice that rose up from the streets, singing
And dying little by little into the distance,
Seized my heart fiercely, as it seizes still.

EDWIN MORGAN

ALLA LUNA

O graziosa luna, io mi rammento
Che, or volge l'anno, sovra questo colle
Io venia pien d'angoscia a rimirarti:
E tu pendevi allor su quella selva
Siccome or fai, che tutta la rischiari.
Ma nebuloso e tremulo dal pianto
Che mi sorgea sul ciglio, alle mie luci
Il tuo volto appariva, che travagliosa
Era mia vita: ed è, né cangia stile,
O mia diletta luna. E pur mi giova
La ricordanza, e il noverar l'etate
Del mio dolore. Oh come grato occorre
Nel tempo giovanil, quando ancor lungo
La speme e breve ha la memoria il corso,
Il rimembrar delle passate cose,
Ancor che triste, e che l'affanno duri!

LA VITA SOLITARIA

La mattutina pioggia, allor che l'ale
Battendo esulta nella chiusa stanza
La gallinella, ed al balcon s'affaccia
L'abitante de' campi, e il Sol che nasce
I suoi tremuli rai fra le cadenti
Stille saetta, alla capanna mia
Dolcemente picchiando, mi risveglia;
E sorgo, e i lievi nugoletti, e il primo
Degli augelli susurro, e l'aura fresca,
E le ridenti piagge benedico:

TO THE MOON

Oh gracious moon, now as the year turns,
I remember how, heavy with sorrow,
I climbed this hill to gaze on you,
And then as now you hung above those trees
Illuminating all. But to my eyes
Your face seemed clouded, tremulous
From the tears that rose beneath my lids,
So painful was my life: and is, my
Dearest moon; its tenor does not change.
And yet, memory and numbering the epochs
Of my grief is pleasing to me. How welcome
In that youthful time—when hope's span is long,
And memory short—is the remembrance even of
Past sad things whose pain endures.

MURIEL KITTEL

THE SOLITARY LIFE

The morning rain! —while the young cooped-up hen
Hops about its prison, flapping its wings,
And the countryman comes to his balcony
And looks out, and the rising sun shoots
Quivering rays among the shower-drops as they
Fall: and softly pattering upon
My cabin roof, rain is the sound I wake to;
I get up, and I bless the light thin clouds
And the first twitter of birds and the breathing
Air and the smiling face of the hills:

Poiché voi, cittadine infauste mura,
Vidi e conobbi assai, là dove segue
Odio al dolor compagno; e doloroso
Io vivo, e tal morrò, deh tosto! Alcuna
Benché scarsa pietà pur mi dimostra
Natura in questi lochi, un giorno oh quanto
Verso me più cortese! E tu pur volgi
Dai miseri lo sguardo; e tu sdegnando
Le sciagure e gli affanni, alla reina
Felicità servi, o natura. In cielo,
In terra amico agl'infelici alcuno
E rifugio non resta altro che il ferro.

Talor m'assido in solitaria parte,
Sovra un rialto, al margine d'un lago
Di taciturne piante incoronato.
Ivi, quando il meriggio in ciel si volve,
La sua tranquilla imago il Sol dipinge,
Ed erba o foglia non si crolla al vento,
E non onda incresparsi, e non cicala
Strider, né batter penna augello in ramo,
Né farfalla ronzar, né voce o moto
Da presso né da lunge odi né vedi.
Tien quelle rive altissima quiete;
Ond'io quasi me stesso e il mondo obblio
Sedendo immoto; e già mi par che sciolte
Giaccian le membra mie, né spirito o senso
Più le commova, e lor quiete antica
Co' silenzi del loco si confonda.

Amore, amore, assai lungi volasti
Dal petto mio, che fu sì caldo un giorno,
Anzi rovente. Con sua fredda mano
Lo strinse la sciaura, e in ghiaccio è volto
Nel fior degli anni. Mi sovvien del tempo

For I have seen and known you, O too much,
Black city walls where pain and hatred follow
Hatred and pain; and in unhappiness
I live, and so will die, soon, soon! Nature
perhaps shows some faint pity still to me
In this place, but how different it was once,
How good, how long ago! For you too turn
Your face from misery; you too, despising
Our disasters, our anxieties, O nature,
Kneel at the throne of happiness. No sky,
No earth yields luckless man a single friend
Or leaves him an escape except cold steel.

I sit sometimes in a lonely place,
On rising ground, at the edge of a lake
Ringed with majestic soundless trees. And there,
When midday rolls across the sky, the sun
Mirrors its painted and unmoving image,
And no wind shakes a grass-blade or a leaf,
And no wave ripples, and no grasshopper
Chirps, not a flutter on the branches
Or even whir of butterfly—no sound,
No stir I hear or see in all this place.
These banks enclose a flawless stillness, and
To me as I sit motionless there the world
And I myself seem fading into oblivion,
Already I see my limbs dissolved, no movement
Or soul or feeling left, their ancient stillness
Diffused in those pervasive silences.

Love, love, you have flown off so far
From my heart: it once was warm for you,
Not warm but ardent. With its cold hand
Misfortune seized it, it is turned to ice
In the flower of my years. My breast remembers

Che mi scendesti in seno. Era quel dolce
E irrevocabil tempo, allor che s'apre
Al guardo giovanil questa infelice
Scena del mondo, e gli sorride in vista
Di paradiso. Al garzoncello il core
Di vergine speranza e di desio
Balza nel petto; e già s'accinge all'opra
Di questa vita come a danza o gioco
Il misero mortal. Ma non sì tosto,
Amor, di te m'accorsi, e il viver mio
Fortuna avea già rotto, ed a questi occhi
Non altro convenia che il pianger sempre.
Pur se talvolta per le piagge apriche,
Su la tacita aurora o quando al sole
Brillano i tetti e i poggi e le campagne,
Scontro di vaga donzelletta il viso;
O qualor nella placida quiete
D'estiva notte, il vagabondo passo
Di rincontro alle ville soffermando,
L'erma terra contemplo, e di fanciulla
Che all'opre di sua man la notte aggiunge
Odo sonar nelle romite stanze
L'arguto canto; a palpitar si move
Questo mio cor di sasso: ahi, ma ritorna
Tosto al ferreo sopor; ch'è fatto estrano
Ogni moto soave al petto mio.

O cara luna, al cui tranquillo raggio
Danzan le lepri nelle selve; e duolsi
Alla mattina il cacciator, che trova
L'orme intricate e false, e dai covili
Error vario lo svia; salve, o benigna
Delle notti reina. Infesto scende
Il raggio tuo fra macchie e balze o dentro
A deserti edifici, in su l'acciaro

The day you entered it. It was that dear,
That unrecapturable time when youth
Looks out at the unfolding scene of this
Unlucky world and that world wears a smile
Like paradise. The young lad's virgin heart,
His purest hope and longing beat and leap
Within his breast; already the poor clay
Girds itself to meet the work of living
As if life was a dance, a game. —But I,
O love, had hardly known you when my life
Was crushed by fate: even then; and then these eyes
Were fitted only for a haunt of tears.
Yet there are times upon the bright hill-slopes,
At silent daybreak and when the sunlight
Pours down the roofs and the low hills and the fields,
And I catch sight of a young girl's sweet face;
Or there will come a summer night made still
With peace, when I have sauntered on, and paused
Among the country houses, watching wide
Over the lonely land, and hear a girl
Weave her fine thread of song as she works on,
Adding the night to day, in empty rooms;
And then I feel this stony heart of mine
Begin to tremble: but oh, it soon returns
To its old iron sleep, for every pulse
Of gentle hope is exiled from my breast.

Dear moon, dear spell of moonlight, the hares
Dance in the spellbound woods; at dawn the hunter
Curses what he finds, tracks crossed and tangled
To lead him astray, and he is led astray
And misses all their lairs: I welcome you,
Night queen, good queen. Unwelcome to some:
When your beam lights up crags and thickets, or falls
Through ruined buildings on the white-faced brigand's

Del pallido ladron ch'a teso orecchio
Il fragor delle rote e de' cavalli
Da lungi osserva o il calpestio de' piedi
Su la tacita via; poscia improvviso
Col suon dell'armi e con la rauca voce
E col funereo ceffo il core agghiaccia
Al passegger, cui semivivo e nudo
Lascia in breve tra' sassi. Infesto occorre
Per le contrade cittadine il bianco
Tuo lume al drudo vil, che degli alberghi
Va radendo le mura e la secreta
Ombra seguendo, e resta, e si spaura
Delle ardenti lucerne e degli aperti
Balconi. Infesto alle malvage menti,
A me sempre benigno il tuo cospetto
Sarà per queste piagge, ove non altro
Che lieti colli e spaziosi campi
M'apri alla vista. Ed ancor io soleva,
Bench'innocente io fossi, il tuo vezzoso
Raggio accusar negli abitati lochi,
Quand'ei m'offriva al guardo umano, e quando
Scopriva umani aspetti al guardo mio.
Or sempre loderollo, o ch'io ti miri
Veleggiar tra le nubi, o che serena
Dominatrice dell'etereo campo,
Questa flebil riguardi umana sede.
Me spesso rivedrai solingo e muto
Errar pe' boschi e per le verdi rive,
O seder sovra l'erbe, assai contento
Se core e lena a sospirar m'avanza.

Knife-blade, where he cocks an ear for the telltale
Rumble of wheels far off, or horses' hoofs
Or tramp of footsteps on the silent road:
Ready without warning and with startling clash
Of steel and with his hideous voice
And grisly churchyard looks to freeze the blood
Of the traveller and to leave him lying soon
Stripped and half-dead on the rocks. Unwelcome too
In city streets: when your white gleam embraces
The lecherous adventurer as he drifts
Sidling by the house-walls, clings to shadows,
Stops in the darkness, goes in fear of every
Streaming open balcony and the blazing
Of the lamps. Unwelcome to black-minded souls—
But O to me your face is always kind
And always will be, over those slopes you light
Before my eyes, those happy hills and fields
You open and unfold. And yet I once attacked
Your beams and beauty—innocent as I was—
When they brought light to thronged and busy places
Uncovering my face to curious looks,
Uncovering others' faces to my own.
But now I can only praise that light, whether
I watch you sailing the clouds, or looking down
In tranquil dominance from your ethereal plains
Upon this home of man so fit for tears.
You will see me many times, silent, alone,
Wandering by the woods and the green banks
Or sitting on the grass, happy enough
If I have heart and spirit left to sigh.

EDWIN MORGAN

ALLA SUA DONNA

Cara beltà che amore
Lunge m'inspiri o nascondendo il viso,
Fuor se nel sonno il core
Ombra diva mi scuoti,
O ne' campi ove splenda
Più vago il giorno e di natura il riso;
Forse tu l'innocente
Secol beasti che dall'oro ha nome,
Or leve intra la gente
Anima voli? o te la sorte avara
Ch'a noi t'asconde, agli avvenir prepara?

Viva mirarti omai
Nulla spene m'avanza;
S'allor non fosse, allor che ignudo e solo
Per novo calle a peregrina stanza
Verrà lo spirto mio. Già sul novello
Aprir di mia giornata incerta e bruna,
Te viatrice in questo arido suolo
Io mi pensai. Ma non è cosa in terra
Che ti somigli; e s'anco pari alcuna
Ti fosse al volto, agli atti, alla favella,
Saria, così conforme, assai men bella.

Fra contanto dolore
Quanto all'umana età propose il fato,
Se vera e quale il mio pensier ti pinge,
Alcun t'amasse in terra, a lui pur fora
Questo viver beato:
E ben chiaro vegg'io siccome ancora
Seguir loda e virtù qual ne' prim'anni
L'amor tuo mi farebbe. Or non aggiunse

TO HIS LADY

Gentle beauty, who with love
inspires me from afar, though near your face is hid,
save when, image divine,
you thrill my heart in sleep,
or in the fields
where nature's smile beams most and day is handsomer;
once perhaps you blessed
the so-called golden age of innocence,
and now, ethereal soul,
you flit among mankind? or does begrudging fate,
hiding you from us, reserve you for a future date?

By now I have no hope
to see your living form;
unless perhaps one of these years my soul,
when stripped and lone, over an untrod path
shall reach an unfamiliar distant land.
Once at the dawn of my uncertain, gloomy days,
I fancied you a fellow-traveler
on this sterile soil. But nothing on this earth
resembles you; and even if one were your like
in countenance, in gesture, and in voice,
though she be so similar, she would be much less fair.

Despite the sorrow
fate assigned to human kind, if someone
should love you on earth in your true essence,
such as my mind pictures you, for him this life
would still seem rapturous:
and I can clearly see how love for you
might prompt me yet to follow praise and virtue
as in my youngest years. But heaven

Il ciel nullo confrorto ai nostri affanni;
E teco la mortal vita saria
Simile a quella che nel cielo india.

Per le valli, ove suona
Del faticoso agricoltore il canto,
Ed io seggo e mi lagno
Del giovanile error che m'abbandona;
E per li poggi, ov'io rimembro e piagno
I perduti desiri, e la perduta
Speme de' giorni miei; di te pensando,
A palpitar mi sveglio. E potess'io,
Nel secol tetro e in questo aer nefando,
L'alta specie serbar; che dell'imago,
Poi che del ver m'è tolto, assai m'appago.

Se dell'eterne idee
L'una sei tu, cui di sensibil forma
Sdegni l'eterno senno esser vestita,
E fra caduche spoglie
Provar gli affanni di funerea vita;
O s'altra terra ne' superni giri
Fra' mondi innumerabili t'accoglie,
E più vaga del Sol prossima stella
T'irraggia, e più benigno etere spiri;
Di qua dove son gli anni infausti e brevi,
Questo d'ignoto amante inno ricevi.

AL CONTE CARLO PEPOLI

Questo affannoso e travagliato sonno
Che noi vita nomiam, come sopporti,

has bestowed no comfort on our miseries;
and mortal life with you would bear
resemblance to the bliss that deifies in heaven.

Along the valleys,
where the tired tiller's song resounds,
and where I sit and moan
my youth's illusions which abandon me;
and along the hills, where I recall
with tears the vanished hopes and lost desires
of earlier years; at the thought of you
my heart awakes revived. And would I might preserve
your lofty image, in this dusky age
and this envenomed air; for since I am deprived
of your true self, I would find comfort in your vision.

If you are one of those
eternal ideas, refused the vesture
of bodily form by eternal wisdom,
along with the submission
of the pains of life foredoomed in fragile frames;
or if your home is in another earth
mid the supernal whirl of countless worlds,
illumined by a nearby star more splendent
than the sun, and if you breathe a kinder ether;
from down here where our years are ominous
and brief, receive this hymn from an unknown adorer.

JEAN-PIERRE BARRICELLI

TO COUNT CARLO PEPOLI

This wearisome and travail-tortured sleep
That we call life, how do you bring yourself,

Pepoli mio? di che speranze il core
Vai sostentando? in che pensieri in quanto
O gioconde o moleste opre dispensi
L'ozio che ti lasciàr gli avi remoti,
Grave retaggio e faticoso? È tutta,
In ogni umano stato, ozio la vita,
Se quell'oprar, quel procurar che a degno
Obbietto non intende, o che all'intento
Giunger mai non potria, ben si conviene
Ozioso nomar. La schiera industre
Cui franger glebe o curar piante e greggi
Vede l'alba tranquilla e vede il vespro,
Se oziosa dirai, da che sua vita
È per campar la vita, e per sé sola
La vita all'uom non ha pregio nessuno,
Dritto e vero dirai. Le notti e i giorni
Tragge in ozio il nocchiero; ozio il perenne
Sudar nelle officine, ozio le vegghie
Son de' guerrieri e il perigliar nell'armi;
E il mercatante avaro in ozio vive:
Che non a sé, non ad altrui, la bella
Felicità, cui solo agogna e cerca
La natura mortal, veruno acquista
Per cura o per sudor, vegghia o periglio.
Pure all'aspro desire onde i mortali
Già sempre infin dal dì che il mondo nacque
D'esser beati sospiraro indarno,
Di medicina in loco apparecchiate
Nella vita infelice avea natura
Necessità diverse, a cui non senza
Opra e pensier si provvedesse, e pieno,
Poi che lieto non può, corresse il giorno
All'umana famiglia; onde agitato
E confuso il desio, men loco avesse
Al travagliarne il cor. Così de' bruti

My Pepoli, to bear it? With what hopes
Is your heart sustained? What meditations, what
Pleasing or tedious labors while away
That leisure wherewith your ancestors endowed you,
Inheritance heavy, burdensome? All life,
In any human station, is idleness
If work which serves no worthy end
Nor can attain its purposed end be named
Rightly mere idleness. That drudging troop
That ploughs the earth and tends the crops and herds,
Whom morning and twilight discover still at toil,
If called mere idlers whose lives ceaselessly
Are spent maintaining life, whereas, thus spent
Upon itself alone, existence is worthless,
Were truly named. The mariner wears out
In idleness his nights and days; the workman
Sweats in perennial idleness; the soldier
At watch, in battle's perils, yet is idle;
The avaricious merchant's trade is idle;
Not for himself or others can man gain
What mortal nature solely yearns for, toils for—
Felicity—purchased through no expense
Of sweat or perils passed or night-long vigils.
But for that unappeased sharp urgency
That since the birth day of the world has driven
All men to sigh in vain for happiness,
Nature devises as a medicine
In this distempered life many diverse
Necessities so that no day may lack
For the human family sufficiency
Of labor and of thought, that all mankind
If they may not be happy may at least
Be ever busy; thus through agitation
And harsh perplexity, desire less keenly
May wring the heart. The animals as well,

La progenie infinita, a cui pur solo,
Né men vano che a noi, vive nel petto
Desio d'esser beati; a quello intenta
Che a lor vita è mestier, di noi men tristo
Condur si scopre e men gravoso il tempo,
Né la lentezza accagionar dell'ore.
Ma noi, che il viver nostro all'altrui mano
Provveder commettiamo, una più grave
Necessità, cui provveder non puote
Altri che noi, già senza tedio e pena
Non adempiam: necessitate, io dico,
Di consumar la vita: improba, invitta
Necessità, cui non tesoro accolto,
Non di greggi dovizia, o pingui campi,
Non aula puote e non purpureo manto
Sottrar l'umana prole. Or s'altri, a sdegno
I vòti anni prendendo, e la superna
Luce odiando, l'omicida mano,
I tardi fati a prevenir condotto,   .
In se stesso non torce; al duro morso
Della brama insanabile che invano
Felicità richiede, esso da tutti
Lati cercando, mille inefficaci
Medicine procaccia, onde quell'una
Cui natura apprestò, mal si compensa.

Lui delle vesti e delle chiome il culto
E degli atti e dei passi, e i vani studi
Di cocchi e di cavalli, e le frequenti
Sale, e le piazze romorose, e gli orti,
Lui giochi e cene e invidiate danze
Tengon la notte e il giorno; a lui dal labbro
Mai non si parte il riso; ahi, ma nel petto,
Nell'imo petto, grave, salda, immota
Come colonna adamantina, siede

Those numberless species, have one single prompting,
No less in vain than ours, within their breasts—
Thirst of felicity; obsessed with that
Sole guidance known to them, they lead,
We see, existences more unafflicted
Than man's, nor need upbraid the slow-paced hours.
But we who into others' hands commit
Provision of mere necessities of life,
A yet more grave necessity that we
Cannot consign to others must ourselves
Assume with all its weight and tedium:
That grave necessity, I mean, of living
Life to the end—uncompromising, stern
Necessity, from which no treasure hoarded,
No plenty of herds or wealth of spreading fields,
No palace or mantle of royal purple may
Free us unquiet mortals. Now if one,
In scorn of empty years, hating the light
Of heaven, is tempted to anticipate
Too tardy death but would not on himself
Turn homicidal hands—envenomed still,
Incurably bitten by the urge to find
Fulfilment of joy, he seeks on every side
Laboriously, forever, fruitlessly,
And tries a thousand nostrums which can yield
No healing, which ill compensate for that
One remedy by Nature's self accorded.

A cult of vesture, of hair-dress, of posture
And carriage see him make, pursue in vain
Coaches and horses, join the intimates
Of salons, haunters of loud public squares,
In gambling-venture, suppers, dances spending
Both night and day, with laughter on his lips
Always; but hidden in his heart, alas,

Noia immortale, incontro a cui non puote
Vigor di giovanezza, e non la crolla
Dolce parola di rosato labbro,
E non lo sguardo tenero, tremante,
Di due nere pupille, il caro sguardo,
La più degna del ciel cosa mortale.

Altri, quasi a fuggir vôlto la trista
Umana sorte, in cangiar terre e climi
L'età spendendo, e mari e poggi errando,
Tutto l'orbe trascorre, ogni confine
Degli spazi che all'uom negl'infiniti
Campi del tutto la natura aperse,
Peregrinando aggiunge. Ahi ahi, s'asside
Su l'alte prue la negra cura, e sotto
Ogni clima, ogni ciel, si chiama indarno
Felicità, vive tristezza e regna.

Havvi chi le crudeli opre di marte
Si elegge a passar l'ore, e nel fraterno
Sangue la man tinge per ozio; ed havvi
Chi d'altrui danni si conforta, e pensa
Con far misero altrui far sé men tristo,
Sì che nocendo usar procaccia il tempo.
E chi virtute o sapienza ed arti
Perseguitando; e chi la propria gente
Conculcando e l'estrane, o di remoti
Lidi turbando la quiete antica
Col mercatar, con l'armi, e con le frodi,
La destinata sua vita consuma.

Te più mite desio, cura più dolce
Regge nel fior di gioventù, nel bello
April degli anni, altrui giocondo e primo
Dono del ciel, ma grave, amaro, infesto
A chi patria non ha. Te punge e move

Deep in his deepest self, a solid weight
Immovable as a column of adamant,
Sits throned undying Ennui, whom the vigor
Of youth cannot avail to shake, nor even
Sweet words that rosy lips may utter, nor
The tender, tremulous glance, the glance of love
From two dark eyes, of things of cumbered earth
The thing most worthy of the heights of heaven.

Another, as if to turn his back on man's
Hard fate, in change of countries, climates, spends
His lease of life, and wanders seas and mountains,
Traverses the orb of earth, through all extent
Of space that Nature yields to man in endless
Expanse makes pilgrimage. Alas, alas,
High on the prow forever sits black care;
Under all weathers, skies, man's happiness
Lies always elsewhere; sorrow lives and reigns.

Others elect to pass the hours in dreadful
Labors of Mars and steep their hands in blood
Of kindred creatures, scourged by ennui; some,
Who can assuage in others' misery
Their own, would find relief inflicting pain
And seek to squander lives enacting evil.
Some by pursuit of wisdom or of virtue
Or arduous arts, and some by trampling under
Their countrymen and foreign folk or rendering
The ancient quiet of remotest shores
By commerce, by loud war or wicked fraud,
Exhaust allotted terms of their existence.

You milder hopes, more gentle cares, control
In blossom of youth, the April prime of being,
To others heaven's first, most jocund gift

Studio de' carmi e di ritrar parlando
Il bel che raro e scarso e fuggitivo
Appar nel mondo, e quel che più benigna
Di natura e del ciel, fecondamente
A noi la vaga fantasia produce,
E il nostro proprio error. Ben mille volte
Fortunato colui che la caduca
Virtù del caro immaginar non perde
Per volger d'anni; a cui serbare eterna
La gioventù del cor diedero i fati;
Che nella ferma e nella stanca etade,
Così come solea nell'età verde,
In suo chiuso pensier natura abbella,
Morte, deserto avviva. A te conceda
Tanta ventura il ciel; ti faccia un tempo
La favilla che il petto oggi ti scalda,
Di poesia canuto amante. Io tutti
Della prima stagione i dolci inganni
Mancar già sento, e dileguar dagli occhi
Le dilettose immagini, che tanto
Amai, che sempre infino all'ora estrema
Mi fieno, a ricordar, bramate e piante.
Or quando al tutto irrigidito e freddo
Questo petto sarà, né degli aprichi
Campi il sereno e solitario riso,
Né degli augelli mattutini il canto
Di primavera, né per colli e piagge
Sotto limpido ciel tacita luna
Commoverammi il cor; quando mi fia
Ogni beltate o di natura o d'arte,
Fatta inanime e muta; ogni alto senso,
Ogni tenero affetto, ignoto e strano;
Del mio solo conforto allor mendico,
Altri studi men dolci, in ch'io riponga
L'ingrato avanzo della ferrea vita,

But somber, bitter, threatening to him
Who has no fatherland. Ardor of song
Inspires you, the desire by fitting words
To frame such beauty as appears to few,
Seldom and transiently, which, more benign
Than heaven and nature, errant fancy shows
Or innate powers illusory evoke
Unnumbered. Many thousand times is blest
He who as years accumulate retains
What may be fleeting, energies of dear
Imagination, for whom the fates preserve
Unquenched perpetual youth within the heart,
Who at the height of manhood, in late age,
As he was wont in years of vernal promise,
In deeps of his thought makes nature beautiful,
Gives death and the desert life. Heaven grant to you
Such gracious fortune; may aspiring flames
Today within your heart warm you with love
Of poetry till you grow gray. Already
I see the sweet mirages of the season
Of youth dissolve; ecstatic images
So dear to me that to my ultimate breath
I shall remember them and yearn, in tears,
For them, departed. And when my heart shall be
Rigid, congealed; when neither sunlit meadows
Serenely smiling in solitude, nor birds
At daybreak chanting of spring, nor a silent moon
In limpid skies above the hills and seashore
Can melt my soul; when loveliness in art
Or nature is inanimate and mute
To me; when tender affections, high emotions
Are alien, strange—beggared of my sole joy
I then shall turn to studies far less cherished
In which the remnants of an iron life
May be consumed. Then truths, blind destinies

Eleggerò. L'acerbo vero, i ciechi
Destini investigar delle mortali
E dell'eterne cose; a che prodotta,
A che d'affanni e di miserie carca
L'umana stirpe; a quale ultimo intento
Lei spinga il fato e la natura; a cui
Tanto nostro dolor diletti o giovi;
Con quali ordini e leggi a che si volva
Questo arcano universo; il qual di lode
Colmano i saggi, io d'ammirar son pago.

In questo specolar gli ozi traendo
Verrò: che conosciuto, ancor che tristo,
Ha suoi diletti il vero. E se del vero
Ragionando talor, fieno alle genti
O mal grati i miei detti o non intesi,
Non mi dorrò, che già del tutto il vago
Desio di gloria antico in me fia spento;
Vana Diva non pur, ma di fortuna
E del fato e d'amor, Diva più cieca.

A SILVIA

Silvia, rimembri ancora
Quel tempo della tua vita mortale,
Quando beltà splendea
Negli occhi tuoi ridenti e fuggitivi,
E tu, lieta e pensosa, il limitare
Di gioventù salivi?

Sonavan le quiete
Stanze, e le vie dintorno,
Al tuo perpetuo canto,

Of mortal and immortal things, I shall
Investigate, why man has been conceived
To bear the unendurable, toward what
Intent at last nature and fate compel us,
What Being takes in our extreme distress
Delight or satisfaction, by what laws
And principles this unintelligible
Creation revolves, a universe the sages
Fill with their praise, a sheer enigma to me.

In these inquiries I shall wear away
My idle days: enlightenment, though sad,
May have delights. And if sometimes, as I
Discourse of truths, my words appear to many
Incomprehensible, intolerable,
I shall not ache with pain; before that time
The hunger of old for fame will be quite spent—
Fame is a deity defiled, more blind
Than ever was Fortune, Love, or Destiny!

DWIGHT DURLING

TO SYLVIA

Sylvia, do you still remember
The days of your mortal life,
When beauty burned in your eyes,
In your laughing elusive eyes,
And gaily, thoughtfully, you touched
Youth's threshold?

The quiet rooms,
And all the paths around,
Rang with your constant song;

Allor che all'opre femminili intenta
Sedevi, assai contenta
Di quel vago avvenir che in mente avevi.
Era il maggio odoroso: e tu solevi
Così menare il giorno.

Io gli studi leggiadri
Talor lasciando e le sudate carte,
Ove il tempo mio primo
E di me si spendea la miglior parte,
D'in su i veroni del paterno ostello
Porgea gli orecchi al suon della tua voce
Ed alla man veloce
Che percorrea la faticosa tela.
Mirava il ciel sereno,
Le vie dorate e gli orti,
E quinci il mar da lungi, e quindi il monte.
Lingua mortal non dice
Quel ch'io sentiva in seno.

Che pensieri soavi,
Che speranze, che cori, o Silvia mia!
Quale allor ci apparia
La vita umana e il fato!
Quando sovviemmi di cotanta speme,
Un affetto mi preme
Acerbo e sconsolato,
E tornami a doler di mia sventura.
O natura, o natura,
Perché non rendi poi
Quel che prometti allor? perché di tanto
Inganni i figli tuoi?

Tu pria che l'erbe inaridisse il verno,
Da chiuso morbo combattuta e vinta,

While intent upon your woman's work
You sat, happily
Dreaming of a pleasant future.
It was the fragrant month of May; and so
Your days flowed by.

I would often leave
My pleasant studies and the well-worn pages
Whereon was spent the best part
Of my youth and of myself,
And from the balconies of my father's house
I would listen eagerly for the sound of your voice,
For the swift movement of your hand
Across the wearisome loom.
I would gaze at the peaceful sky,
At the gardens and the golden paths,
At the mountains on one side, on the other the far-off sea.
No mortal words can tell
The feelings of my heart.

What pleasant thoughts we had,
My dearest Sylvia, what hopes and loves!
How fine the life and destiny of man
Seemed to us then!
Now the remembrance of those high hopes
Plunges me into bitter
Unconsolable despair,
And I turn again to mourn my wretched life.
Ah Nature, Nature,
Why do you not fulfil
Your early promises? Why do you deceive
Your sons so bitterly?

Before winter withered the grasses,
Hidden sickness fought and conquered you,

Perivi, o tenerella. E non vedevi
Il fior degli anni tuoi;
Non ti molceva il core
La dolce lode or delle negre chiome,
Or degli sguardi innamorati e schivi;
Né teco le compagne ai dì festivi
Ragionavan d'amore.

Anche peria fra poco
La speranza mia dolce: agli anni miei
Anche negaro i fati
La giovanezza. Ahi come,
Come passata sei,
Cara compagna dell'età mia nova,
Mia lacrimata speme!
Questo è quel mondo? questi
I diletti, l'amor, l'opre, gli eventi
Onde cotanto ragionammo insieme?
Questa la sorte dell'umane genti?
All'apparir del vero
Tu, misera, cadesti: e con la mano
La fredda morte ed una tomba ignuda
Mostravi di lontano.

LE RICORDANZE

Vaghe stelle dell'Orsa, io non credea
Tornare ancor per uso a contemplarvi
Sul paterno giardino scintillanti,
E ragionar con voi dalle finestre
Di questo albergo ove abitai fanciullo,

My delicate Sylvia: you died,
And never saw
The flowering of your years.
None softened your heart
With praise, sweet praise of raven hair,
Of loving bashful glances.
No holiday companions
Talked to you of love.

My fair hopes died too
Soon after; and the Fates
Also denied my years
Their youth. Ah, how
Completely have you vanished,
Dear companion of my earliest age:
My wept-for hope!
Is this that world, these
The delights, love, labors and events
We talked of so much together?
Is this man's fate?
At the coming of truth
You fell, poor wretched one; and cold death
And a naked tomb your hand
Showed me from afar.

MURIEL KITTEL

MEMORIES

Fair stars of the Bear, I never thought
I should return again to gaze on you
Sparkling above my father's garden, as of
Old, and commune with you from the window
Of this house where I passed my boyhood,

E delle gioie mie vidi la fine.
Quante immagini un tempo, e quante fole
Creommi nel pensier l'aspetto vostro
E delle luci a voi compagne! allora
Che, tacito, seduto in verde zolla,
Delle sere io solea passar gran parte
Mirando il cielo, ed ascoltando il canto
Della rana rimota alla campagna!
E la lucciola errava appo le siepi
E in su l'aiuole, susurrando al vento
I viali odorati, ed i cipressi
Là nella selva; e sotto al patrio tetto
Sonavan voci alterne, e le tranquille
Opre de' servi. E che pensieri immensi,
Che dolci sogni mi spirò la vista
Di quel lontano mar, quei monti azzurri,
Che di qua scopro, e che varcare un giorno
Io mi pensava, arcani mondi, arcana
Felicità fingendo al viver mio!
Ignaro del mio fato, e quante volte
Questa mia vita dolorosa e nuda
Volentier con la morte avrei cangiato.

Né mi diceva il cor che l'età verde
Sarei dannato a consumare in questo
Natio borgo selvaggio, intra una gente
Zotica, vil; cui nomi strani, e spesso
Argomento di riso e di trastullo,
Son dottrina e saper; che m'odia e fugge,
Per invidia non già, che non mi tiene
Maggior di sé, ma perché tale estima
Ch'io mi tenga in cor mio, sebben di fuori
A persona giammai non ne fo segno.
Qui passo gli anni, abbandonato, occulto,
Senz'amor, senza vita; ed aspro a forza
Tra lo stuol de' maleviol divengo:

And where I saw my happiness end.
How many and how foolish were the images
The sight of you and your companion stars
Created in my thought! Then it was,
That sitting silently on the green turf,
I would pass a large part of the night
Watching the sky, and listening to the song of
Frogs, distant in the countryside;
The firefly then would wander along the hedge
And over the flower-beds; while the fragrant
Alleys and the cypresses in the wood
Whispered to the wind. Under my father's
Roof were heard successive voices, and quiet
Tasks of servants. But what vast thoughts,
What pleasant dreams were inspired in me
By the sight of the far-off sea and those azure hills
That I discovered then, and thought one day
To cross, inventing secret worlds
And secret happiness for my life to come—
Not knowing then my fate, nor how often
I would willingly have exchanged for death
This sorrowful and barren life of mine.

Nor did my heart tell me that my green years
Would be condemned to wither in this barbarous
Town, where I was born, among a base and
Uncouth race, for whom knowledge and learning
Bear a strange repute (often indeed a cause
For sport and laughter); a race that hates and shuns me,
Nor yet from envy, or because they think me
Better than themselves, but because I think
Myself so in my heart, although I never
Openly showed this to anyone. Here,
Deserted and obscure, I pass the years,
Bereft of love and life; and perforce
Grow bitter among the malicious crowd.

Qui di pietà mi spoglio e di virtudi,
E sprezzator degli uomini mi rendo,
Per la greggia ch'ho appresso: e intanto vola
Il caro tempo giovanil; più caro
Che la fama e l'allor, più che la pura
Luce del giorno, e lo spirar: ti perdo
Senza un diletto, inutilmente, in questo
Soggiorno disumano, intra gli affanni,
O dell'arida vita unico fiore.

Viene il vento recando il suon dell'ora
Dalla torre del borgo. Era conforto
Questo suon, mi rimembra, alle mie notti,
Quando fanciullo, nella buia stanza,
Per assidui terrori io vigilava,
Sospirando il mattin. Qui non è cosa
Ch'io vegga o senta, onde un'immagin dentro
Non torni, e un dolce rimembrar non sorga.
Dolce per sé; ma con dolor sottentra
Il pensier del presente, un van desio
Del passato, ancor tristo, e il dire: io fui.
Quella loggia colà, volta agli estremi
Raggi del dì; queste dipinte mura,
Quei figurati armenti, e il Sol che nasce
Su romita campagna, agli ozi miei
Porser mille diletti allor che al fianco
M'era, parlando, il mio possente errore
Sempre, ov'io fossi. In queste sale antiche,
Al chiaror delle nevi, intorno a queste
Ampie finestre sibilando il vento,
Rimbombaro i sollazzi e le festose
Mie voci al tempo che l'acerbo, indegno
Mistero dell cose a noi si mostra
Pien di dolcezza; indelibata, intera
Il garzoncel, come inesperto amante,

I strip myself of piety and virtue,
And here become a hater of mankind
As these sheep have taught me; meanwhile
The dear time of youth flies away,
Dearer than fame or laurel crown, than the clear
Light of day or breath itself; I lose you
Without one delight, futilely,
In anguish, in this inhuman place,
Only flower of our barren life!

The wind comes, bearing the chiming of
The hour from the town belfry. This sound
Brought comfort to me, I remember,
When as a child I lay awake at night,
Besieged by terrors in my darkened room,
Longing for morning. Here is nothing
That I see or hear that does not bring back
A former image, or evoke some sweet remembrance.
Sweet in itself; but then painfully creeps in
The thought of the present, and a futile longing
For the past, though sad, and the words: I was.
The loggia there, facing the last
Beams of daylight; these painted walls,
Those drawings of herds, and the sun rising over
The solitary landscape—all offered
Myriad delights to my idle hours, when still
Spoke at my side my strong delusion,
Always, wherever I went. These old rooms,
In the light of the snow's brightness, while
The wind whistled at the ample windows,
Reverberated with my games and cheerful
Talk at the time of life when the harsh, pernicious
Mystery of things shows itself to us
Full of sweetness; like a green lover,
The boy gazes amorously at his fickle

La sua vita ingannevole vagheggia,
E celeste beltà fingendo ammira.

O speranze, speranze; ameni inganni
Della mia prima età! sempre, parlando,
Ritorno a voi; che per andar di tempo,
Per variar d'affetti e di pensieri,
Obbliarvi non so. Fantasmi, intendo,
Son la gloria e l'onor; diletti e beni
Mero desio; non ha la vita un frutto,
Inutile miseria. E sebben vòti
Son gli anni miei, sebben deserto, oscuro
Il mio stato mortal, poco mi toglie
La fortuna, ben veggo. Ahi, ma qualvolta
A voi ripenso, o mie speranze antiche,
Ed a quel caro immaginar mio primo;
Indi riguardo il viver mio sì vile
E sì dolente, e che la morte è quello
Che di cotanta speme oggi m'avanza;
Sento serrarmi il cor, sento ch'al tutto
Consolarmi non so del mio destino.
E quando pur questa invocata morte
Sarammi allato, e sarà giunto il fine
Della sventura mia; quando la terra
Mi fia straniera valle, e dal mio sguardo
Fuggirà l'avvenir; di voi per certo
Risovverrammi; e quell'imago ancora
Sospirar mi farà, farammi acerbo
L'esser vissuto indarno, e la dolcezza
Del dì fatal tempererà d'affanno.

E già nel primo giovanil tumulto
Di contenti, d'angosce e di desio,
Morte chiamai più volte, e lungamente
Mi sedetti colà su la fontana

Life, that is still untouched and whole, and feigns
Celestial beauty that he marvels at.

Ah my hopes, my hopes, pleasing illusions
Of my early years! Always, in talking,
I come back to you, for, despite Time's
Passing, despite change in thought and feeling,
I cannot forget you. Phantoms, I see now,
Are fame and honor; things pleasant and good
Are merely wishes; life bears no fruit, but is
Only futile suffering. And although empty
Are my years, although barren and obscure
My mortal state, Fortune deprives me of little:
This I clearly see. Ah, but whenever
I think again of you, my early hopes,
And you, first dear dreams of youth,
And then look at my life, so base,
So painful, and see that death is all that today
Remains of such great hope, I feel my heart
Contract, I feel I cannot be entirely
Reconciled unto my destiny.
And yet, when this longed-for death is at
My side, and the end of my misfortunes
Has arrived; when the earth becomes an alien
Valley to me, and the future flees
Beyond my vision, I shall surely then
Remember you; and your image still
Will make me sigh with longing, will embitter
This existence spent in vain, and the sweetness
Of that fatal day will mix with pain.

Yet already, in the first youthful
Turmoil of pleasure, anguish and desire,
I would often summon death, and sat
For long hours by the fountain there,

Pensoso di cessar dentro quell'acque
La speme e il dolor mio. Poscia, per cieco
Malor, condotto della vita in forse,
Piansi la bella giovanezza, e il fiore
De' miei poveri dì, che sì per tempo
Cadeva: e spesso all'ore tarde, assiso
Sul conscio letto, dolorosamente
Alla fioca lucerna poetando,
Lamentai co' silenzi e con la notte
Il fuggitivo spirto, ed a me stesso
In sul languir cantai funereo canto.

Chi rimembrar vi può senza sospiri,
O primo entrar di giovinezza, o giorni
Vezzosi, inenarrabili, allor quando
Al rapito mortal primieramente
Sorridon le donzelle; a gara intorno
Ogni cosa sorride; invidia tace,
Non desta ancora ovver benigna; e quasi
(Inusitata maraviglia!) il mondo
La destra soccorrevole gli porge,
Scusa gli errori suoi, festeggia il novo
Suo venir nella vita, ed inchinando
Mostra che per signor l'accolga e chiami?
Fugaci giorni! a somigliar d'un lampo
Son dileguati. E qual mortale ignaro
Di sventura esser può, se a lui già scorsa
Quella vaga stagion, sì il suo buon tempo,
Se giovanezza, ahi giovanezza, è spenta?

O Nerina! e di te forse non odo
Questi luoghi parlar? caduta forse
Dal mio pensier sei tu? Dove sei gita,
Che qui sola di te la ricordanza
Trovo, dolcezza mia? Più non ti vede

Thinking of ending, underneath those waters,
Both hope and sorrow. Afterwards, when
Blind sickness brought me in danger of
My life, I mourned my fair youth, and the flower
Of my poor days that so untimely fell;
And often at a late hour, sitting
On my sympathetic bed, sorrowfully
Versifying by the faint lamp,
I mourned in silence and in darkness
The fleeing spirit, and for my failing life
Sang to myself a funeral song.

Who can remember you without regret,
O first beginnings of youth, O lovely
Days defying description, when maidens
Smile for the first time at enraptured
Man, and everything in sight vies
To smile on him; envy is silent,
Unawakened yet, or else benign:
It is as if the world—unwonted marvel—
Extends its right hand to give him help,
Forgives his errors, celebrates his first
Arrival at life's door, and bows before him,
To make him welcome and to call him lord.
Fleeting days! They disappear like a
Lightning flash. And what man can be
Ignorant of misfortune, if that fair season
Has fled from him already, if his best years,
His youth—ah youth—has been extinguished?

O Nerina, do not these surroundings
Speak to me of you? Can you have vanished
From my thought? Where can you have gone,
My sweet one, that memories are all
That are left for me to find? Your native soil

Questa Terra natal: quella finestra,
Ond'eri usata favellarmi, ed onde
Mesto riluce delle stelle il raggio,
È deserta. Ove sei, che più non odo
La tua voce sonar, siccome un giorno,
Quando soleva ogni lontano accento
Del labbro tuo, ch'a me giungesse, il volto
Scolorarmi? Altro tempo. I giorni tuoi
Furo, mio dolce amor. Passasti. Ad altri
Il passar per la terra oggi è sortito,
E l'abitar questi odorati colli.
Ma rapida passasti; e come un sogno
Fu la tua vita. Ivi danzando; in fronte
La gioia ti splendea, splendea negli occhi
Quel confidente immaginar, quel lume
Di gioventù, quando spegneali il fato,
E giacevi. Ahi Nerina! In cor mi regna
L'antico amor. Se a feste anco talvolta,
Se a radunanze io movo, infra me stesso
Dico: o Nerina, a radunanze, a feste
Tu non ti acconci più, tu più non movi.
Se torna maggio, e ramoscelli e suoni
Van gli amanti recando alle fanciulle,
Dico: Nerina mia, per te non torna
Primavera giammai, non torna amore.
Ogni giorno sereno, ogni fiorita
Piaggia ch'io miro, ogni goder ch'io sento,
Dico: Nerina or più non gode; i campi,
L'aria non mira. Ahi tu passasti, eterno
Sospiro mio: passasti: e fia compagna
D'ogni mio vago immaginar, di tutti
I miei teneri sensi, i tristi e cari
Moti del cor, la rimembranza acerba.

Sees you no more: that window
Where you were wont to speak to me, where
Sad starlight glitters now, is
Empty. Where are you? For I no longer hear
The echo of your voice—when once every
Distant accent from your lips that
Reached my ears would make my face turn
Pale. That was another era. Your days
Are past, my gentle love. You have gone:
It is given to others now to walk the earth,
And dwell among these fragrant hills.
But you went swiftly: your life was
Like a dream. Dancing you went, on your brow
Happiness shone, and shining in your eyes
Was the confident vision, and the light
Of youth, when fate extinguished them, and
Struck you down. Ah Nerina! The old love
Still sways my heart. If I go at times
To festivals and gatherings, I say,
Murmuring to myself: Ah Nerina,
You come no more, no more you deck yourself
For gatherings or festivals. When May
Comes again, when with sprigs and song
Lovers go singing to their girls,
I say: Nerina mine, for you Spring
Will never come again, nor love come more.
Each fair calm day, each flowering
Slope I see, each pleasure that I feel,
I say: Nerina has no further joy in this;
The fields, the air she cannot see. Ah,
You are gone, my eternal sigh:
You are gone, and for companion to all
My fair illusions, to all my tender feelings
All the dear and sad emotions of my
Heart, you leave me bitter memory.   MURIEL KITTEL

CANTO NOTTURNO
DI UN PASTORE ERRANTE DELL'ASIA

Che fai tu, luna, in ciel? dimmi, che fai,
Silenziosa luna?
Sorgi la sera, e vai,
Contemplando i deserti; indi ti posi.
Ancor non sei tu paga
Di riandare i sempiterni calli?
Ancor non prendi a schivo, ancor sei vaga
Di mirar queste valli?
Somiglia alla tua vita
La vita del pastore.
Sorge in sul primo albore;
Move la greggia oltre pel campo, e vede
Greggi, fontane ed erbe;
Poi stanco si riposa in su la sera:
Altro mai non ispera.
Dimmi, o luna: a che vale
Al pastor la sua vita,
La vostra vita a voi? dimmi: ove tende
Questo vagar mio breve,
Il tuo corso immortale?

Vecchierel bianco, infermo,
Mezzo vestito e scalzo,
Con gravissimo fascio in su le spalle,
Per montagna e per valle,
Per sassi acuti, ed alta rena, e fratte,
Al vento, alla tempesta, e quando avvampa
L'ora, e quando poi gela,
Corre via, corre, anela,
Varca torrenti e stagni,
Cade, risorge, e più e più s'affretta,

poems aways comparing
author to object of Nature

NOCTURNE
OF A WANDERING SHEPHERD IN ASIA

What do you do in the sky, tell me what,
Most silent moon?
You rise at evening and go
To contemplate the deserts; then you rest.
Have you not had your fill
Of crossing and recrossing the sempiternal ways?
Are you still unwearied, still content
To gaze upon these valleys?
Like unto your life
Is the life of a shepherd.
He rises at earliest dawn,
Moves his flock far over the fields, and sees
Flocks, fountains, pastures;
Then weary, towards evening he takes his rest:
He never hopes for change.
Tell me moon, of what use
Is his life to the shepherd,   *depressing*
Or your life to you? Whither lead
This brief wandering of mine
And your immortal course?

Old, shrunken, whitehaired, ill,
Barefoot, half-clothed,
Bearing on his shoulders a grievous load,
Over valleys and hills,
Over sharp rocks, deep sand, through briars,
Through winds and storms, through weather that burns
With heat and after turns to ice,
Breathless, man rushes, rushes,
Across torrents, through bogs he goes,
Falls, rises again, pushes himself to greater speed,

Senza posa o ristoro,
Lacero, sanguinoso; infin ch'arriva
Colà dove la via
E dove il tanto affaticar fu volto:
Abisso orrido, immenso,
Ov'ei precipitando, il tutto obblia.
Vergine luna, tale
È la vita mortale.

Nasce l'uomo a fatica,
Ed è rischio di morte il nascimento.
Prova pena e tormento
Per prima cosa; e in sul principio stesso
La madre e il genitore
Il prende a consolar dell'esser nato.
Poi che crescendo viene,
L'uno e l'altro il sostiene, e via pur sempre
Con atti e con parole
Studiasi fargli core,
E consolarlo dell'umano stato:
Altro ufficio più grato
Non si fa da parenti alla lor prole.
Ma perché dare al sole,
Perché reggere in vita
Chi poi di quella consolar convenga?
Se la vita è sventura,
Perché da noi si dura?
Intatta luna, tale
È lo stato mortale.
Ma tu mortal non sei,
E forse del mio dir poco ti cale.

Pur tu, solinga, eterna peregrina,
Che sì pensosa sei, tu forse intendi,
Questo viver terreno,

With no rest, no comfort,
But wounds and blood; until at last he reaches
That point at which his path
And all his colossal toil were aimed:
And into an abyss,
Dreadful and immense, he falls to reach oblivion.
This, oh virgin moon,
This is man's life.

Man is born with labor,
And birth itself is at the risk of death.
Suffering and pain are proved
The earliest realities; and from that starting point
His mother and father undertake
To console him for his birth.
As he comes to grow
They both support him, and continually
Strive by word and deed
To give him courage,
To console him for his human state.
There is no better thing
That parents can offer their children.
But why bring into the world,
Why sustain life
In him who afterwards must be consoled?
If life is misfortune
Why do we endure?
Moon undefiled,
Such is mortal life.
Yet you are not mortal,
And little care, perhaps, to hear me speak.

But you, solitary, eternal wanderer,
Perhaps you, so full of thought, may understand
This earthly life,

Il patir nostro, il sospirar, che sia;
Che sia questo morir, questo supremo
Scolorar del sembiante,
E perir dalla terra, e venir meno
Ad ogni usata, amante compagnia.
E tu certo comprendi
Il perché delle cose, e vedi il frutto
Del mattin, della sera,
Del tacito, infinito andar del tempo.
Tu sai, tu certo, a qual suo dolce amore
Rida la primavera,
A chi giovi l'ardore, e che procacci
Il verno co' suoi ghiacci.
Mille cose sai tu, mille discopri,
Che son celate al semplice pastore.
Spesso quand'io ti miro
Star così muta in sul deserto piano,
Che, in suo giro lontano, al ciel confina;
Ovver con la mia greggia
Seguirmi viaggiando a mano a mano;
E quando miro in cielo arder le stelle;
Dico fra me pensando:
A che tante facelle?
Che fa l'aria infinita, e quel profondo
Infinito seren? che vuol dir questa
Solitudine immensa? ed io che sono?
Così meco ragiono: e della stanza
Smisurata e superba,
E dell'innumerabile famiglia;
Poi di tanto adoprar, di tanti moti
D'ogni celeste, ogni terrena cosa,
Girando senza posa,
Per tornar sempre là donde son mosse;
Uso alcuno, alcun frutto
Indovinar non so. Ma tu per certo,

And what our sighing, what our suffering mean;
What death is, what this last
Fading of our features
As we perish from the earth, and vanish
From all familiar, loving faces.
You must understand
The why of things, and see the fruit
Of dawn and nightfall,
Of Time's silent, infinite passage.
You know, you must know, for what sweet love
The Springtime smiles,
Whom Summer's heat makes glad, and what the frosts
Of winter serve.
A thousand things you know, a thousand more
Discover that are hid from simple shepherds.
Often, as I gaze on you
Hanging so still above the empty plain,
That in its distant sweep borders the sky;
Or see you following me as I move
Slowly, gradually with my flock;
Or as I gaze at the burning stars of heaven,
I commune with my thought, seeking
The reason for all that brilliance,
The purpose of infinite space and the deep
Infinity of the heavens, the meaning
Of that immense solitude, and what I am.
These things I ponder; and the dwelling,
Boundless and superb,
And the innumerable host;
Then the vast working, the many motions
Of all heavenly, all earthly things,
All spinning without rest,
Always to return there whence they came:
Whether there be any purpose,
Any profit, I cannot guess. But you,

Giovinetta immortal, conosci il tutto.
Questo io conosco e sento,
Che degli eterni giri,
Che dell'esser mio frale,
Qualche bene o contento
Avrà fors'altri; a me la vita è male.

O greggia mia che posi, oh te beata
Che la miseria tua, credo, non sai!
Quanta invidia ti porto!
Non sol perché d'affanno
Quasi libera vai;
Ch'ogni stento, ogni danno,
Ogni estremo, timor subito scordi;
Ma più perché giammai tedio non provi.
Quando tu siedi all'ombra, sovra l'erbe,
Tu se' queta e contenta;
E gran parte dell'anno
Senza noia consumi in quello stato.
Ed io pur seggo sovra l'erbe, all'ombra,
E un fastidio m'ingombra
La mente, ed uno spron quasi mi punge
Sì che, sedendo, più che mai son lunge
Da trovar pace o loco.
E pur nulla non bramo,
E non ho fino a qui cagion di pianto.
Quel che tu goda o quanto,
Non so già dir; ma fortunata sei.
Ed io godo ancor poco,
O greggia mia, né di ciò sol mi lagno.
Se tu parlar sapessi, io chiederei:
Dimmi: perché giacendo
A bell'agio, ozioso,
S'appaga ogni animale;
Me, s'io giaccio ni riposo, il tedio assale?

Immortal maid, must know these things.
This I know and feel,
Whatever is good and happy
In the eternal motions,
In my frail existence,
Another perhaps shall find; life to me is evil.

How fortunate are you, my flock, as you rest there,
Your unhappiness I believe you cannot know.
How much I envy you!
Not only because you live
Almost free of trouble,
And can immediately forget
All hurt, all misery, all shock of fear,
But more that boredom never touches you.
Sitting on the grass in the shade,
You are peaceful and content;
Nearly the whole year
You spend in that untroubled way.
But I have only to sit in the shade on the grass,
And a bitter weariness engulfs
My mind, and a spur seems to goad me
While I sit, for more than ever am I far
From finding rest or peace.
And yet I want nothing,
Nor do I now have cause for tears.
What is it you enjoy, how great your pleasure,
I cannot tell, but you are fortunate.
And though I have little pleasure,
This my flock, is not my sole complaint.
If you could speak, I would ask you why
It is that lying
Idle, at perfect ease,
Satisfies all animals,
When boredom seizes me if I lie down to rest.

Forse s'avess'io l'ale
Da volar su le nubi,
E noverar le stelle ad una ad una,
O come il tuono errar di giogo in giogo,
Più felice sarei, dolce mia greggia,
Più felice sarei, candida luna.
O forse erra dal vero,
Mirando all'altrui sorte, il mio pensiero:
Forse in qual forma, in quale
Stato che sia, dentro covile o cuna,
È funesto a chi nasce il dì natale.

LA QUIETE DOPO LA TEMPESTA

Passata è la tempesta:
Odo augelli far festa, e la gallina,
Tornata in su la via,
Che ripete il suo verso. Ecco il sereno
Rompe là da ponenta, alla montagna;
Sgombrasi la campagna,
E chiaro nella valle il fiume appare.
Ogni cor si rallegra, in ogni lato
Risorge il romorio,
Torna il lavoro usato.
L'artigiano a mirar l'umido cielo,
Con l'opra in man, cantando,
Fassi in su l'uscio; a prova
Vien fuor la femminetta a còr dell'acqua
Della novelle piova;
E l'erbaiuol rinnova
Di sentiero in sentiero

Perhaps if I had wings
To fly above the clouds
And number off the stars one by one,
Or wander like the thunder from peak to peak,
I would be happier, gentle flock,
I would be happier, oh pure white moon.
Or, gazing at another's lot,
Perhaps my thought wanders from the truth:
Perhaps in any form, under any
Condition, whether in den or cradle,
The day of birth is mournful for him who is born.

MURIEL KITTEL

THE CALM AFTER THE STORM

I hear the end of the storm
As the birds strike up their song, and then the hen
Ventures on the road again,
Repeating its quiet note. See how the sky
Breaks up, goes blue behind the western heights!
The countryside grows bright,
The stream shines clear across the valley floor.
Every heart rejoices, on every side
The day's work comes to life,
A hum is heard once more.
The workman looks out singing at his door,
And gazes, work in hand,
At the glistening sky; the women
Come hurrying to be first to draw the water
Left by the new sweet rain;
The fruit-seller passes by
As before, from lane to lane

Il grido giornaliero.
Ecco il Sol che ritorna, ecco sorride
Per li poggi e le ville. Apre i balconi,
Apre terrazzi e logge la famiglia:
E, dalla via corrente, odi lontano
Tintinnio di sonagli; il carro stride
Del passegger che il suo cammin ripiglia.

Si rallegra ogni core.
Sì dolce, sì gradita
Quand'è, com'or, la vita?
Quando con tanto amore
L'uomo a' suoi studi intende?
O torna all'opre? o cosa nova imprende?
Quando de' mali suoi men si ricorda?
Piacer figlio d'affanno;
Gioia vana, ch'è frutto
Del passato timore, onde si scosse
E paventò la morte
Chi la vita abborria;
Onde in lungo tormento,
Fredde, tacite, smorte,
Sudàr le genti e palpitàr, vedendo
Mossi alle nostre offese
Folgori, nembi e vento.

O natura cortese,
Son questi i doni tuoi,
Questi i diletti sono
Che tu porgi ai mortali. Uscir di pena
È diletto fra noi.
Pene tu spargi a larga mano; il duolo
Spontaneo sorge: e di piacer, quel tanto
Che per mostro e miracolo talvolta
Nasce d'affanno, è gran guadagno. Umana

Crying his daily refrain.
See how the sun has come back, see how it smiles
On the roofs and the hills! Servants throw open
Balconies and terraces and galleries; below,
Bells are heard jingling on the far highway;
The carriage creaks as it resumes the miles
The traveller begins again to go.

It rejoices every heart.
And when is life so sweet
As now, or so complete?
When does man show such art
And love in the labor of his hands?—
Picking up old threads, or searching for new strands?
When is he less conscious of his troubles?
Pleasure, born of suffering:
Joy, empty: the fruit
Of a terror that has passed, and passing, shaken
With fear of death the man
Who once abhorred his life:
A long inquisition, frightening
People to shiver and sweat
Speechless and cold and pale in impending strife
Visibly gathered against us,
Wind and cloud and lightning.

Charitable nature! These
Are the gifts you have to give,
These are the happinesses
You offer mortal men. The end of pain
We take as happiness.
Pain you have scattered with both hands; sorrow
Grows without effort; such pleasure as is born
At times by miracle, a prodigy cradled
In grief, becomes our greatest gain. O breed

Prole cara agli eterni! assai felice
Se respirar ti lice
D'alcun dolor: beata
Se te d'ogni dolor morte risana.

IL SABATO DEL VILLAGGIO

La donzelletta vien dalla campagna,
In sul calar del sole,
Col suo fascio dell'erba; e reca in mano
Un mazzolin di rose e di viole,
Onde, siccome suole,
Ornare ella si appresta
Dimani, al dì di festa, il petto e il crine.
Siede con le vicine
Su la scala a filar la vecchierella,
Incontro là dove si perde il giorno;
E novellando vien del suo buon tempo,
Quando ai dì della festa ella si ornava,
Ed ancor sana e snella
Solea danzar la sera intra di quei
Ch'ebbe compagni dell'età più bella.
Già tutta l'aria imbruna,
Torna azzurro il sereno, e tornan l'ombre
Giù da' colli da' tetti,
Al biancheggiar della recente luna.
Or la squilla dà segno
Della festa che viene;
Ed a quel suon diresti
Che il cor si riconforta.
I fanciulli gridando

Of men eternally dear! happy indeed
If you have breathing-space
From pain: blessed all the more
If death should heal you of the pain you fear!

EDWIN MORGAN

VILLAGE SATURDAY

Now as the sun goes down the young girl comes
Home from the fields, with grass
In a bundle and carrying in her hand
A rose and violet nosegay for her dress
And hair tomorrow, to face
Tomorrow's holiday
With a festive beauty, as the custom is.
The worn old woman sits
With neighbors on the stair, sits spinning, glancing
Out where the day's last light is disappearing,
Recalling stories of the good old times
When she too would put on her holiday best
And would be dancing, dancing
The whole night through, in her supple days of youth,
In the midst of the lads who found her—then!—entrancing.
Already the air grows dark,
A clear deep blue the sky, and shadows slipping
Already from hills and roofs
That whiten underneath a young moon's arc.
Now by a sharp peal of bells
The festive day is signalled;
The sound comes over like
A reassurance of the heart.
The children with their cries

Su la piazzuola in frotta,
E qua e là saltando,
Fanno un lieto romore:
E intanto riede alla sua parca mensa,
Fischiando, il zappatore,
E seco pensa al dì del suo riposo.

Poi quando intorno è spenta ogni altra face,
E tutto l'altro tace,
Odi il martel picchiare, odi la sega
Del legnaiuol, che veglia
Nella chiusa bottega alla lucerna,
E s'affretta, e s'adopra
Di fornir l'opra anzi chiarir dell'alba.

Questo di sette è il più gradito giorno,
Pien di speme e di gioia:
Diman tristezza e noia
Recheran l'ore, ed al travaglio usato
Ciascuno in suo pensier farà ritorno.

Garzoncello scherzoso,
Cotesta età fiorita
È come un giorno d'allegrezza pieno,
Giorno chiaro, sereno,
Che precorre alla festa di tua vita.
Godi, fanciullo mio; stato soave,
Stagion lieta è cotesta.
Altro dirti non vo'; ma la tua festa
Ch'anco tardi a venir non ti sia grave.

As they crowd the tiny square
Jumping here, running there,
Turn joy into a sound:
While the farm worker with his hoe returns,
Whistling, to his meagre meal,
And thinks how his one day of rest comes round.

Then, when all the surrounding lights are out,
With silence round about,
You hear the tapping hammer, hear the saw
Of the joiner still awake
Behind the shutters of his shop, working
Furiously by lanternlight
To finish his job before the brightening dawn.

Of all the seven, this day is most favored—
Filled with a happy hope:
Tomorrow's hours will stop
On sadness, disenchantment, the return
Of every mind to its familiar labors.

Lad's life of joy! Your
Manhood buds full.
How like a day it is, swelled tight with gladness,
A pure day in its brightness
Unfolding to your earthly festival!
Be happy, boy; such moments are like grace,
Their state is sweet. From me
No further words; but may you never see
Your long-sought festal day with different face.

EDWIN MORGAN

CORO DI MORTI

Sola nel mondo eterna, a cui si volve
Ogni creata cosa,
In te, morte, si posa
Nostra ignuda natura;
Lieta no, ma sicura
Dall'antico dolor. Profonda notte
Nella confusa mente
Il pensier grave oscura;
Alla speme, al desio, l'arido spirto
Lena mancar si sente:
Così d'affanno e di temenza è sciolto,
E l'età vote e lente
Senza tedio consuma.

Vivemmo: e qual di paurosa larva,
E di sudato sogno,
A lattante fanciullo erra nell'alma
Confusa ricordanza:
Tal memoria n'avanza
Del viver nostro: ma da tema è lunge
Il rimembrar. Che fummo?
Che fu quel punto acerbo
Che di vita ebbe nome?
Cosa arcana e stupenda
Oggi è la vita al pensier nostro, e tale
Qual de' vivi al pensiero
L'ignota morte appar. Come da morte
Vivendo rifuggia, così rifugge
Dalla fiamma vitale
Nostra ignuda natura;
Lieta no ma sicura,
Però ch'esser beato
Nega ai mortali e nega a' morti il fato.

CHORUS OF THE DEAD

Alone on earth eternal, to whom does come
Every created thing,
In you, Death, reposes
Our naked natural being,
Not joyful, but secure
From ancient sorrow. Deepest night
Within the confusèd mind
All weighty thought does darken.
To hope, to desire, the dried-up spirit
Feels its energy waning.
Thus from unease and fear it is released,
And the slow and empty ages
It spends unwearied.

We lived: and as the fearful spectre
And the sweated dream
Wanders in the soul of the suckling child,
A confused remembrance,
So remains the memory
Of our lifetime; but far from fear
Is our remembering. What were we?
What was that bitter point
That had the name of life?
An awesome and mysterious thing
Life seems to our thoughts today. And
Such to living minds
Does unknown death appear. As from death
It fled while living, so flees
From the vital flame
Our naked natural being,
Not joyful, but secure,
For to be blessed
Is denied to mortals, denied to the dead by Fate.

MURIEL KITTEL

IL PENSIERO DOMINANTE

Dolcissimo, possente
Dominator di mia profonda mente;
Terribile, ma caro
Dono del ciel; consorte
Ai lùgubri miei giorni,
Pensier che innanzi a me sì spesso torni.

Di tua natura arcana
Chi non favella? il suo poter fra noi
Chi non sentì? Pur sempre
Che in dir gli effetti suoi
Le umane lingue il sentir proprio sprona,
Par novo ad ascoltar ciò ch'ei ragiona.

Come solinga è fatta
La mente mia d'allora
Che tu quivi prendesti a far dimora!
Ratto d'intorno intorno al par del lampo
Gli altri pensieri miei
Tutti si dileguàr. Siccome torre
In solitario campo,
Tu stai solo, gigante, in mezzo a lei.

Che divenute son, fuor di te solo,
Tutte l'opre terrene,
Tutta intera la vita al guardo mio!
Che intollerabil noia
Gli ozi, i commerci usati,
E di vano piacer la vana spene,
Allato a quella gioia,
Gioia celeste che da te mi viene!

SOVEREIGN THOUGHT

Powerful, most kind
sovereign of my innermost mind;
terrible, yet precious
gift of heaven; consort
of my dismal days,
thought, so oft recurring to my gaze.

Who does not speak
of your mysterious nature? and who among us
has not felt its power? Yet always,
when men's private feelings
prompt their tongues give utterance to its passioned ways,
the theme we hear seems ever new to us.

How solitary
is my mind become
since in it first you made your home!
As swiftly as a lightning flash and all about me
my other thoughts
dispersed. Just like a tower
on a lonesome lea,
You stand alone, gigantic, in your power.

Of what meaning to me now
are all the earth's affairs,
the whole of life itself, apart from you!
How intolerably tedious
seem daily intercourse,
the idle hours, and the vain hopes of vain pleasures,
when to that joy compared,
celestial joy that you transmit to me!

Come da' nudi sassi
Dello scabro Apennino
A un campo verde che lontan sorrida
Volge gli occhi bramoso il pellegrino;
Tal io dal secco ed aspro
Mondano conversar vogliosamente,
Quasi in lieto giardino, a te ritorno,
E ristora i miei sensi il tuo soggiorno.

Quasi incredibil parmi
Che la vita infelice e il mondo sciocco
Già per gran tempo assai
Senza te sopportai;
Quasi intender non posso
Come d'altri desiri,
Fuor ch'a te somiglianti, altri sospiri.

Giammai d'allor che in pria
Questa vita che sia per prova intesi,
Timor di morte non mi strinse il petto.
Oggi mi pare un gioco
Quella che il mondo inetto,
Talor lodando, ognora abborre e trema,
Necessitade estrema;
E se periglio appar, con un sorriso
Le sue minacce a contemplar m'affiso.

Sempre i codardi, e l'alme
Ingenerose, abbiette
Ebbi in dispregio. Or punge ogni atto indegno
Subito i sensi miei;
Move l'alma ogni esempio
Dell'umana viltà subito a sdegno.
Di questa età superba,
Che di vote speranze si nutrica,

As from the naked rocks
of a scraggy Apennine
the pilgrim turns his pining eye
to a green plain smiling from afar;
so with eagerness
from wry, malicious converse with the world,
as to a lovely garden, I return
to you, to heal my soul in this sojourn.

It scarce seems credible
that I could bear so long a time without you
this wretched life
and foolish world;
I scarce can see why
other men should sigh
for yearnings not resembling you.

Never, from the hour
when first experience taught me what life is,
did fear of death constrain my breast.
That ultimate necessity
today appears a jest,
while by the inept world, if sometimes praised,
it still is feared, abhorred;
and if danger comes, I contemplate intent
its every menace with a smile.

Always I have despised
coward, ignoble,
abject souls. Now each unworthy act
stings me at once with rage;
each deed of human vileness
moves at once my feelings to disdain.
To this proud age
which feeds on empty hopes,

Vaga di ciance, e di virtù nemica;
Stolta, che l'util chiede,
E inutile la vita
Quindi più sempre divenir non vede;
Maggior mi sento. A scherno
Ho gli umani giudizi; e il vario volgo
A' bei pensieri infesto,
E degno tuo disprezzator, calpesto.

A quello onde tu movi,
Quale affetto non cede?
Anzi qual altro affetto
Se non quell'uno intra i mortali ha sede?
Avarizia, superbia, odio, disdegno,
Studio d'onor, di regno,
Che sono altro che voglie
Al paragon di lui? Solo un affetto
Vive tra noi: quest'uno,
Prepotente signore,
Dieder l'eterne leggi all'uman core.

Pregio non ha, non ha ragion la vita
Se non per lui, per lui ch'all'uomo è tutto;
Sola discolpa al fato,
Che noi mortali in terra
Pose a tanto patir senz'altro frutto;
Solo per cui talvolta,
Non alla gente stolta, al cor non vile
La vita della morte è più gentile.

Per còr le gioie tue, dolce pensiero,
Provar gli umani affanni,
E sostener molt'anni
Questa vita mortal, fu non indegno;
Ed ancor tornerei,

absorbed in trifles, virtue's enemy,
which, fool-like, asks the useful,
and does not see
how life thereby grows more useless,
I feel superior. I condemn
human judgments; and the motley crew
that scorns all lofty thoughts,
your due disparager, I trample under foot.

What passion does not yield
to that from which you stem?
Indeed what other passion,
save this one, holds reign in mortal hearts?
Ambition, avarice, disdain, and hate,
the cult of praise and kingdom,
are these not appetites
compared with this? Only one passion
rules within: this one was sent,
a lord omnipotent,
to the human heart by the eternal laws.

Except for this, for this which to mankind is all,
life has no worth and holds no meaning;
it alone justifies fate,
that placed us down on earth
to suffer so and with no other blessing;
through it alone at times,
not stupid minds, but hearts refined
may feel that life can be more kind than death.

To cull your joys, O gentle thought,
it was not worthless
to suffer human pain
and many years this mortal life sustain;
and I would still return,

Così qual son de' nostri mali esperto,
Verso un tal segno a incominciare il corso:
Che tra le sabbie e tra il vipereo morso,
Giammai finor sì stanco
Per lo mortal deserto
Non venni a te, che queste nostre pene
Vincer non mi paresse un tanto bene.

Che mondo mai, che nova
Immensità, che paradiso è quello
Là dove spesso il tuo stupendo incanto
Parmi innalzar! dov'io,
Sott'altra luce che l'usata errando,
Il mio terreno stato
E tutto quanto il ver pongo in obblio!
Tali son, credo, i sogni
Degl'immortali. Ahi finalmente un sogno
In molta parte onde s'abbella il vero
Sei tu, dolce pensiero;
Sogno e palese error. Ma di natura,
Infra i leggiadri errori
Divina sei; perché sì viva e forte,
Che incontro al ver tenacemente dura,
E spesso al ver s'adegua,
Né si dilegua pria, che in grembo a morte.

E tu per certo, o mio pensier, tu solo
Vitale ai giorni miei,
Cagion diletta d'infiniti affanni,
Meco sarai per morte a un tempo spento:
Ch'a vivi segni dentro l'alma io sento
Che in perpetuo signor dato mi sei.
Altri gentili inganni
Soleami il vero aspetto
Più sempre infievolir. Quanto più torno

though I am versed by now in earthly ills,
to repursue the path toward such a goal:
for I never came to you so weary,
in mortal desert through the sands
and viper's deadly bite,
that such a good did not seem to defeat
these greatest sorrows of our birthright.

O what a world,
what new immensity, what paradise is that
to which, by your stupendous wizardry,
I seem to rise! where I,
roaming under other than familiar light,
forget my earthly state
and all the suffering that here is real.
Such are, I feel,
the dreams of the immortal gods. Ah, in the end,
sweet thought, you are in large part but a dream
with which truth is adorned:
a dream and plain illusion. Yet your nature,
mid all our fair illusions,
is divine; for it is so vital and strong,
that with resolve it can resist reality,
and oft seem just as real,
nor does it fade, till in the lap of death.

And surely you, my thought, O you alone
the life-source of my days,
beloved cause of endless woes,
will someday fall with me under the stroke of death:
for in my soul I feel by vivid signs
you are given me as my eternal sovereign.
At the sight of truth
other benign delusions
ever more grow pale. The more I turn

A riveder colei
Della qual teco ragionando io vivo,
Cresce quel gran diletto,
Cresce quel gran delirio, ond'io respiro.
Angelica beltade!
Parmi ogni più bel volto, ovunque io miro,
Quasi una finta imago
Il tuo volto imitar. Tu sola fonte
D'ogni altra leggiadria,
Sola vera beltà parmi che sia.

Da che ti vidi pria,
Di qual mia seria cura ultimo obbietto
Non fosti tu? quanto del giorno è scorso,
Ch'io di te non pensassi? ai sogni miei
La tua sovrana imago
Quante volte mancò? Bella qual sogno,
Angelica sembianza,
Nella terrena stanza,
Nell'alte vie dell'universo intero,
Che chiedo io mai, che spero
Altro che gli occhi tuoi veder più vago?
Altro più dolce aver che il tuo pensiero?

A SE STESSO

Or poserai per sempre,
Stanco mio cor. Perì l'inganno estremo
Ch'eterno io mi credei. Perì. Ben sento,
In noi di cari inganni,
Non che la speme, il desiderio è spento.
Posa per sempre. Assai

to look on her again
through whom I live discoursing with you,
the greater that delight,
the greater that delirium swells by which I breathe.
Angelic loveliness!
Anywhere I gaze, each fairest face
appears a pictured image
copying your visage. You alone are source
of every other grace,
the sole true beauty, it appears to me.

Since I beheld you first,
of what most anxious care of mine have you not been
object supreme? what hour of day has even passed
without some thought of you? how often in my dreams
did your sovereign image
fail to greet me? Lovely as a dream,
angelic semblance,
in these earthly abodes,
upon the total universe's lofty roads,
what may I ever ask,
or hope to see, more beauteous than your eyes?
or ever have more sweet than thought of you?

JEAN-PIERRE BARRICELLI

TO HIMSELF

Now, and for ever, you may rest,
My haggard heart. Dead is that last deception.
I had thought love would be enduring. It is dead.
I know that my hoping, and even
My wishing to be so dearly deceived, have fled.
Rest, and for ever. The strife

Palpitasti. Non val cosa nessuna
I moti tuoi, né di sospiri è degna
La terra. Amaro e noia
La vita, altro mai nulla; e fango è il mondo.
T'acqueta omai. Dispera
L'ultima volta. Al gener nostro il fato
Non donò che il morire. Omai disprezza
Te, la natura, il brutto
Poter che, ascoso, a comun danno impera,
E l'infinita vanità del tutto.

ASPASIA

Torna dinanzi al mio pensier talora
Il tuo sembiante, Aspasia. O fuggitivo
Per abitati lochi a me lampeggia
In altri volti; o per deserti campi,
Al dì sereno, alle tacenti stelle,
Da soave armonia quasi ridesta,
Nell'alma a sgomentarsi ancor vicina
Quella superba vision risorge.
Quanto adorata, o numi, e quale un giorno
Mia delizia ed erinni! E mai non sento
Mover profumo di fiorita piaggia,
Né di fiori olezzar vie cittadine,
Ch'io non ti vegga ancor qual eri il giorno
Che ne' vezzosi appartamenti accolta,
Tutti odorati de' novelli fiori
Di primavera, del color vestita
Della bruna viola, a me si offerse
L'angelica tua forma, inchino il fianco
Sovra nitide pelli, e circonfusa

Has throbbed through you, has throbbed. Nothing is worth
One tremor or one beat; the very earth
Deserves no sign. Life
Has shrunk to dregs and rancor; the world is unclean.
Calm, calm. For this
Is the last despair. What gift has fate brought man
But dying? Now, vanquish in your disdain
Nature and the ugly force
That furtively shapes human ill, and the whole
Infinite futility of the universe.

EDWIN MORGAN

ASPASIA

From time to time your face returns, Aspasia,
To fill my mind. Sometimes, 'mid passing throngs
I see your fleeting likeness in another.
And often, when I tread the lonely heath
By cloudless day or under the still stars,
As if awakened by harmonious silence
Within my soul, near swooning with the charge,
That glorious vision rises once again.
How much adored—o gods—how truly once
My whole delight and torment! Even now
The perfume wafted from a garden bed
Or scent of flowers in the city's streets
Brings back unfailingly the sight of you
As on that day, when in your dainty room,
Suffused from fragrance of fresh blooming buds
Of spring time, seated at your ease and clad
In hue of violet, your angelic form
Was offered me, the curving flank disposed
On gleaming pelts and all was circumfused

D'arcana voluttà; quando tu, dotta
Allettatrice, fervidi sonanti
Baci scoccavi nelle curve labbra
De' tuoi bambini, il niveo collo intanto
Porgendo, e lor di tue cagioni ignari
Con la man leggiadrissima stringevi
Al seno ascoso e desiato. Apparve
Novo ciel, nova terra, e quasi un raggio
Divino al pensier mio. Così nel fianco
Non punto inerme a viva forza impresse
Il tuo braccio lo stral, che poscia fitto
Ululando portai finch'a quel giorno
Si fu due volte ricondotto il sole.

Raggio divino al mio pensiero apparve,
Donna, la tua beltà. Simile effetto
Fan la bellezza e i musicali accordi,
Ch'alto mistero d'ignorati Elisi
Paion sovente rivelar. Vagheggia
Il piagato mortal quindi la figlia
Della sua mente, l'amorosa idea,
Che gran parte d'Olimpo in sé racchiude,
Tutta al volto ai costumi alla favella
Pari alla donna che il rapito amante
Vagheggiare ed amar confuso estima.
Or questa egli non già, ma quella, ancora
Nei corporali amplessi, inchina ed ama.
Alfin l'errore e gli scambiati oggetti
Conoscendo, s'adira; e spesso incolpa
La donna a torto. A quella eccelsa imago
Sorge di rado il femminile ingegno;
E ciò che inspira ai generosi amanti
La sua stessa beltà, donna non pensa
Né comprender potria. Non cape in quelle
Anguste fronti ugual concetto. E male

With dark desire—while you, accomplished temptress,
Arching your snow white neck, pressed resonant
And burning kisses on your children's lips,
With slender arms yet closer drawing them,
Innocent of your purpose, to that breast
Discreetly veiled and dearly coveted.
Oh then within my soul new heavens appeared,
An earth all new, almost a ray divine!
Thus in my not unarmored side your hand
With living force drove in the fatal dart
Which henceforth deep imbedded I did bear,
Crying for pain of it, until the sun
Had twice been led back to that selfsame day.

In very truth your beauty, to my mind,
My lady, seemed a ray divine. Beauty
And musical accords have like effect.
The mystery of unknown Elysiums
It seems, both may reveal. The stricken mortal
Is wont to model then his own mind's child,
The amorous idea, itself comprising
Most of Olympus, after the face and speech
And manner of the woman whom, confused
By rapture, he imagines that he loves.
It is not she but always the idea,
Even when bodies join, he cherishes.
Learning at length his error and the changed
Objects he waxes wroth and often blames
The woman—wrongly. Her intelligence
But rarely rises to that lofty image,
And all that her own beauty may inspire
In generous lover a woman does not know
Nor could she understand; her narrow brow
Affords not scope for such a concept. Vain
Is a man's hope, too easily deceived

Al vivo sfolgorar di quegli sguardi
Spera l'uomo ingannato, e mal richiede
Sensi profondi, sconosciuti, e molto
Più che virili, in chi dell'uomo al tutto
Da natura è minor. Che se più molli
E più tenui le membra, essa la mente
Men capace e men forte anco riceve.

Né tu finor giammai quel che tu stessa
Inspirasti alcun tempo al mio pensiero,
Potesti, Aspasia, immaginar. Non sai
Che smisurato amor, che affanni intensi,
Che indicibili moti e che deliri
Movesti in me; né verrà tempo alcuno
Che tu l'intenda. In simil guisa ignora
Esecutor di musici concenti
Quel ch'ei con mano o con la voce adopra
In chi l'ascolta. Or quell'Aspasia è morta
Che tanto amai. Giace per sempre, oggetto
Della mia vita un dì: se non se quanto,
Pur come cara larva, ad ora ad ora
Tornar costuma e disparir. Tu vivi,
Bella non solo ancor, ma bella tanto,
Al parer mio, che tutte l'altre avanzi.
Pur quell'ardor che da te nacque è spento:
Perch'io te non amai, ma quella Diva
Che già vita, or sepolcro, ha nel mio core.
Quella adorai gran tempo; e sì mi piacque
Sua celeste beltà, ch'io, per insino
Già dal principio conoscente e chiaro
Dell'esser tuo, dell'arti e delle frodi,
Pur ne' tuoi contemplando i suoi begli occhi,
Cupido ti seguii finch'ella visse,
Ingannato non già, ma dal piacere
Di quella dolce somiglianza un lungo
Servaggio ed aspro a tollerar condotto.

By brightly flashing glances, vainly he seeks
Deep, rare and more than virile sentiments
In creatures by their nature less than man
In all things, for as given softer limbs
So are their minds less large and less robust.

Hence all that you yourself inspired in me
Up to this moment, you could not conceive,
Aspasia. What boundless love, what pangs,
What transports, and what wild delirium
You aroused in me you know not, nor will come
Ever a time when you will understand.
So the creator of harmonies knows not
What he induces by his hand or voice
In one who listens. Dead is that Aspasia
Whom I so loved; one day my life's sole purpose
She now lies in her grave forever, save
As, like a cherished ghost, she may at times
Return to fade away again. And you live on
Not only fair, but to my seeming, still
So fair as to surpass all others. But
The ardor born of you is spent and cold,
For you I loved not but the divine form
To which my heart, its tomb now, once gave life.
Her I adored for long, and such delight
I found in her celestial loveliness,
That though I was aware from the first moment
Of your beguiling nature and its arts
Yet still, in your eyes contemplating hers,
While she yet lived I joyed to follow you,
Deceived by no means, but willingly induced
Through pleasure in the likeness to endure
A long and bitter time of servitude.

Vaunt it—as you well may. Go now and tell
How I consented to bow down my head

Or ti vanta, che il puoi. Narra che sola
Sei del tuo sesso a cui plegar sostenni
L'altero capo, a cui spontaneo porsi
L'indomito mio cor. Narra che prima,
E spero ultima certo, il ciglio mio
Supplichevol vedesti, a te dinanzi
Me timido, tremante (ardo in ridirlo
Di sdegno e di rossor), me di me privo,
Ogni tua voglia, ogni parola, ogni atto
Spiar sommessamente, a' tuoi superbi
Fastidi impallidir, brillare in volto
Ad un segno cortese, ad ogni sguardo
Mutar forma e color. Cadde l'incanto,
E spezzato con esso, a terra sparso
Il giogo: onde m'allegro. E sebben pieni
Di tedio, alfin dopo il servire e dopo
Un lungo vaneggiar, contento abbraccio
Senno con libertà. Che se d'affetti
Orba la vita, e di gentili errori,
È notte senza stelle a mezzo il verno,
Già del fato mortale a me bastante
E conforte e vendetta è che su l'erba
Qui neghittoso immobile giacendo,
Il mar la terra e il ciel miro e sorrido.

SOPRA
UN BASSO RILIEVO ANTICO SEPOLCRALE

DOVE UNA GIOVANE MORTA
È RAPPRESENTATA IN ATTO DI PARTIRE,
ACCOMIATANDOSI DAI SUOI

Dove vai? chi ti chiama
Lunge dai cari tuoi,
Bellissima donzella?

To you alone of all your sex, how you
Alone won free surrender of my heart
Erstwhile unconquered. Say you were the first
(And I do hope the last) to see my brow
Bent suppliant, to see me stand before you
Timid and trembling (how I burn with scorn
And shame in the retelling!) aye, beside myself
Submissively alert to all your words
And whims and gestures, paling at your wrath,
Lighting with joy at any gentle sign,
Changing in hue and posture with each glance.
The spell is broken now and shattered lies
My yoke, whence I rejoice. And however both
Be full of tedium, yet content at last
After long slavery and folly I embrace
My wit and freedom. For although a life
Devoid of sweet illusion and of love
Is as a winter night with no star shining
Yet it suffices me as consolation
And recompense for the hard fate of man
That idle, carefree, I lie on the grass
And smiling contemplate shore, sea and sky.

THOMAS G. BERGIN

ON A BAS-RELIEF ON AN ANCIENT TOMB

WHERE A DEAD GIRL
IS SHOWN IN THE ACT OF DEPARTURE,
TAKING LEAVE OF HER FAMILY

Where are you going? Who calls you
Far from your dear ones,
Most lovely maiden?

Sola, peregrinando, il patrio tetto
Sì per tempo abbandoni? a queste soglie
Tornerai tu? farai tu lieti un giorno
Questi ch'oggi ti son piangendo intorno?

Asciutto il ciglio ed animosa in atto,
Ma pur mesta sei tu. Grata la via
O dispiacevol sia, tristo il ricetto
A cui movi o giocondo,
Da quel tuo grave aspetto
Mal s'indovina. Ahi ahi, né già potria
Fermare io stesso in me, né forse al mondo
S'intese ancor, se in disfavore al cielo
Se cara esser nomata,
Se misera tu debbi o fortunata.

Morte ti chiama; al cominciar del giorno
L'ultimo istante. Al nido onde ti parti,
Non tornerai. L'aspetto
De' tuoi dolci parenti
Lasci per sempre. Il loco
A cui movi, è sotterra:
Ivi fia d'ogni tempo il tuo soggiorno.
Forse beata sei; ma pur chi mira,
Seco pensando, al tuo destin, sospira.

Mai non veder la luce
Era, credo, il miglior. Ma nata, al tempo
Che reina bellezza si dispiega
Nelle membra e nel volto
Ed incomincia il mondo
Verso lei di lontano ad atterrarsi;
In sul fiorir d'ogni speranza, e molto
Prima che incontro alla festosa fronte
I lugubri suoi lampi il ver baleni;

Alone, on pilgrimage, your father's roof
Do you so soon relinquish? To this threshhold
Will you return? Will you some day bring joy
To those who, weeping, stand around you now?

Dry are your eyelids, and lively your gestures,
Yet are you sad. Whether pleasant the way
Or distasteful, whether gloomy the shelter
To which you pass, or gay,
From your grave countenance
It's hard to tell. Alas, alas, I could not
Be certain in my mind, nor in the world
May it yet be known, whether in heaven's disfavor
Or love you must be thought,
Whether you are pitiable or fortunate.

Death is calling you; at day's beginning
The last moment comes. The nest you leave
You will not find again. The sight
Of your dear parents
You lose forever. The place
To which you go is underground:
There for all time shall your dwelling be.
You may be blessed; but he who looks at you,
And contemplates your destiny does sigh.

Never to see the light
I think were best. But once born, when
Regal beauty is unfolding
In limb and features,
And the world begins
To come from far to pay its homage to her;
At the flowering of all hope, and long
Before truth against her cheerful brow
Has flashed its sombre lightnings;

Come vapore in nuvoletta accolto
Sotto forme fugaci all'orizzonte,
Dileguarsi così quasi non sorta,
E cangiar con gli oscuri
Silenzi della tomba i dì futuri,
Questo se all'intelletto
Appar felice, invade
D'alta pietade ai più costanti il petto.

Madre temuta e pianta
Dal nascer già dell'animal famiglia,
Natura, illaudabil maraviglia,
Che per uccider partorisci e nutri,
Se danno è del mortale
Immaturo perir, come il consenti
In quei capi innocenti?
Se ben, perché funesta,
Perché sovra ogni male,
A chi si parte, a chi rimane in vita,
Inconsolabil fai tal dipartita?

Misera ovunque miri,
Misera onde si volga, ove ricorra,
Questa sensibil prole!
Piacqueti che delusa
Fosse ancor dalla vita
La speme giovanil; piena d'affanni
L'onda degli anni; ai mali unico schermo
La morte; e questa inevitabil segno,
Questa, immutata legge
Ponesti all'uman corso. Ahi perché dopo
Le travagliose strade, almen la meta
Non ci prescriver lieta? anzi colei
Che per certo futura
Portiam sempre, vivendo, innanzi all'alma,

Like mist gathered in a tiny cloud
In fleeting forms on the horizon's edge,
To be dissolved as though she had not been,
And to exchange for the dark
Silences of the tomb her future days,
Though this to the intellect
Seems happy, it fills
With deepest pity the most steadfast heart.

Mother dreaded and lamented
By the family of creatures from their birth,
Nature, marvel impossible to praise,
Who, but to kill, give birth and nourishment,
If it is harmful for man
To die untimely, why do you allow
It for these innocent heads?
If good, why so tragic,
Why above all evils,
For those who leave this life and those who stay,
Do you make departure unconsolable?

Pitiable wherever they look,
Pitiable where they turn or run,
These sensitive offspring!
It pleased you still
To disappoint by life
The hopes of youth, to fill with sorrows
The tide of years; against our woes as only shield
Set death; and this is the inevitable seal,
This the immutable law
That you have set for human life. Alas, why after
The wearisome roads, could not at least the goal
Prescribed for us be happy? Rather than
The end which, sure to come,
We bear forever while we live before our souls,

Colei che i nostri danni
Ebber solo conforto,
Velar di neri panni,
Cinger d'ombra sì trista,
E spaventoso in vista
Più d'ogni flutto dimostrarci il porto?

Già se sventura è questo
Morir che tu destini
A tutti noi che senza colpa, ignari,
Né volontari al vivere abbandoni,
Certo ha chi more invidiabil sorte
A colui che la morte
Sente de' cari suoi. Che se nel vero,
Com'io per fermo estimo,
Il vivere è sventura,
Grazia il morir, chi però mai potrebbe,
Quel che pur si dovrebbe,
Desiar de' suoi cari il giorno estremo,
Per dover egli scemo
Rimaner di se stesso,
Veder d'in su la soglia levar via
La diletta persona
Con chi passato avrà molt'anni insieme,
E dire a quella addio senz'altra speme
Di riscontrarla ancora
Per la mondana via;
Poi solitario abbandonato in terra,
Guardando attorno, all'ore ai lochi usati
Rimemorar la scorsa compagnia?
Come, ahi come, o natura, il cor ti soffre
Di strappar dalle braccia
All'amico l'amico,
Al fratello il fratello,
La prole al genitore,

Which our injuries
Had as only comfort—
Rather than shroud in black,
Encircle it with shade so sad,
and more terrible to our eyes
Than all the flooding tide reveal the port?

But unfortunate as is
This dying that you decree
For all of us whom, guiltless, unaware,
Against our will, you relegate to living,
Yet he who dies is still more enviable
In lot than he who suffers
The death of his dear ones. If it is true,
As firmly I believe,
That living is misfortune,
And death a kindness, yet who is there who could,
Even if he should,
Wish for his dear ones the final day,
Whereon he must remain
But half himself,
And see carried off across the threshold
The beloved figure
With whom he has spent so many years,
And bid farewell without further hope
Of ever meeting more
On this world's path;
And then alone, forsaken on this earth,
Looking about him, the times and habitual places
Remember of that lost companionship?
How, alas, how Nature, can your heart
Let you wrench a friend
From his friend's arms,
A brother from a brother,
Children from a parent,

All'amante l'amore: e l'uno estinto,
L'altro in vita serbar? Come potesti
Far necessario in noi
Tanto dolor, che sopravviva amando
Al mortale il mortal? Ma da natura
Altro negli atti suoi
Che nostro male o nostro ben si cura.

SOPRA IL RITRATTO DI UNA BELLA DONNA

SCOLPITO NEL MONUMENTO SEPOLCRALE DELLA MEDESIMA

Tal fosti: or qui sotterra
Polve e scheletro sei. Su l'ossa e il fango
Immobilmente collocato invano,
Muto, mirando dell'etadi il volo,
Sta, di memoria solo
E di dolor custode, il simulacro
Della scorsa beltà. Quel dolce sguardo,
Che tremar fe', se, come or sembra, immoto
In altrui s'affisò; quel labbro, ond'alto
Par, come d'urna piena,
Traboccare il piacer; quel collo, cinto
Già di desio; quell'amorosa mano,
Che spesso, ove fu porta,
Sentì gelida far la man che strinse;
E il seno, onde la gente
Visibilmente di pallor si tinse,
Furo alcun tempo: or fango
Ed ossa sei: la vista
Vituperosa e trista un sasso asconde.

The beloved from the lover: and the one deceased,
Keep the other living? How could you
Make obligatory
Such great sorrow that mortal survives mortal
When they love? But Nature in her deeds
To some other end
Than our harm or benefit gives heed.

MURIEL KITTEL

ON THE PORTRAIT OF A BEAUTIFUL LADY
ENGRAVED ON HER SEPULCHRAL MONUMENT

Such you were: who now underground
Are skeleton and dust. Above the bones and dirt,
Immobile and useless, a silent
Witness to the flight of years,
Sole guardian of memory and grief,
Stands this image of past beauty.
That gentle gaze, if bent fixedly on others,
(As it seems now) made them tremble;
That lip, whence deep pleasure seems to over-
Flow, as from a brimming urn; that neck,
Once girt with desire; that loving hand,
That often, where it touched,
Felt the hand it grasped grow chill;
And the breast, whose pallor
Visibly tinged the beholder—
All these once were: and now are only
Dirt and bones; the sad
And infamous sight a tomb conceals.

Così riduce il fato
Qual sembianza fra noi parve più viva
Immagine del ciel. Misterio eterno
Dell'esser nostro. Oggi d'eccelsi, immensi
Pensieri e sensi inenarrabil fonte,
Beltà grandeggia, e pare,
Quale splendor vibrato
Da natura immortal su queste arene,
Di sovrumani fati,
Di fortunati regni e d'aurei mondi
Segno e sicura spene
Dare al mortale stato:
Diman, per lieve forza,
Sozzo a vedere, abominoso, abbietto
Divien quel che fu dianzi
Quasi angelico aspetto,
E dalle menti insieme
Quel che da lui moveva
Ammirabil concetto, si dilegua.

Desiderii infiniti
E visioni altere
Crea nel vago pensiere,
Per natural virtù, dotto concento;
Onde per mar delizioso, arcano
Erra lo spirto umano,
Quasi come a diporto
Ardito notator per l'Oceano:
Ma se un discorde accento
Fere l'orecchio, in nulla
Torna quel paradiso in un momento.

Natura umana, or come,
Se frale in tutto e vile,
Se polve ed ombra sei, tant'alto senti?

Thus does Fate bring low
That form that among us seemed Heaven's
Liveliest image. Eternal mystery
Of our being: today the ineffable source
Of vast, lofty thoughts and feelings,
Beauty grows big, and appears
Like the tremulous glory
Of immortal nature above these shores,
Giving to man's estate
The sign and certain hope
Of superhuman destiny,
Of blessed realms and worlds of gold.
Tomorrow, at a light blow,
It becomes abominable, abject,
Dreadful to behold, that before
Had almost an angel's face;
And that which joined the mind
To inspire it with
Marvelous conceits, has vanished.

Infinite desires
And lofty visions
Are bred in eager thought
By learned harmony's inherent power;
Whence, mysterious, through a delightful sea,
The human spirit wanders,
As a bold swimmer wanders
Through the ocean for his sport;
But if a note of discord
Strike the ear, instantly
That paradise is turned to naught.

Ah, human nature, how
If utterly base and frail,
If dust and shadow, can you feel deep sentiment?

Se in parte anco gentile,
Come i più degni tuoi moti e pensieri
Son così di leggeri
Da sì basse çagioni e desti e spenti?

IL TRAMONTO DELLA LUNA

Quale in notte solinga,
Sovra campagne inargentate ed acque,
Là 've zefiro aleggia,
E mille vaghi aspetti
E ingannevoli obbietti
Fingon l'ombre lontane
Infra l'onde tranquille
E rami e siepi e collinette e ville;
Giunta al confin del cielo,
Dietro Apennino od Alpe, o del Tirreno
Nell'infinito seno
Scende la luna; e si scolora il mondo;
Spariscon l'ombre, ed una
Oscurità la valle e il monte imbruna;
Orba la notte resta,
E cantando, con mesta melodia,
L'estremo albor della fuggente luce,
Che dianzi gli fu duce,
Saluta il carrettier dalla sua via;

Tal si dilegua, e tale
Lascia l'età mortale
La giovinezza. In fuga
Van l'ombre e le sembianze
Dei dilettosi inganni; e vengon meno

If you are yet partly noble
How can your finest impulses and thoughts
Thus so easily,
By such causes, be aroused and spent?

MURIEL KITTEL

THE SETTING OF THE MOON

As in the lonely night,
Over silvered countryside and waters,
Where a light breeze flutters,
And distant shadows form
A thousand vague images
And illusory objects
Among the tranquil waves,
Branches, hedgerows, little hills and houses;
Having reached the limit of the sky,
Beyond Apennine or Alp, or into the
Infinite Tyrrhenian gulf
The moon sinks; and the world fades;
Shadows vanish, valley and mountain
Blend into one dark obscurity;
The night remains, blind,
And singing a mournful tune,
The travelling wagoner salutes
The last glimmer of the fading light
That but now was his guide.

So it vanishes, and so
Youth leaves our mortal
Years. They flee away,
The shadows and appearances
Of sweet illusions; then fade

Le lontane speranze,
Ove s'appoggia la mortal natura.
Abbandonata, oscura
Resta la vita. In lei porgendo il guardo,
Cerca il confuso viatore invano
Del cammin lungo che avanzar si sente
Meta o ragione; e vede
Che a sé l'umana sede,
Esso a lei veramente è fatto estrano.

Troppo felice e lieta
Nostra misera sorte
Parve lassù, se il giovanile stato,
Dove ogni ben di mille pene è frutto,
Durasse tutto della vita il corso.
Troppo mite decreto
Quel che sentenzia ogni animale a morte,
S'anco mezza la via
Lor nor si desse in pria
Della terribil morte assai più dura.
D'intelletti immortali
Degno trovato, estremo
Di tutti i mali, ritrovàr gli eterni
La vecchiezza, ove fosse
Incolume il desio, la speme estinta,
Secche le fonti del piacer, le pene
Maggiori sempre, e non più dato il bene.

Voi, collinette e piagge,
Caduto lo splendor che all'occidente
Inargentava della notte il velo,
Orfane ancor gran tempo
Non resterete; che dall'altra parte
Tosto vedrete il cielo
Imbiancar novamente, e sorger l'alba:

The distant hopes
On which human nature leans.
Forsaken, darkling,
Life remains. Straining his eyes,
The perplexed traveler seeks in vain
On the long road he seems to follow
Some goal or purpose; and perceives
That to the human state itself
He has indeed become a stranger.

Far too happy and joyful
Would seem our wretched lot
To those above, if youthfulness,
When every good is the fruit of myriad pains,
Should last throughout life's course.
Far too mild the decree
That sentences all creatures to death,
Unless half their journey
Is first proved to be
Much harsher than that dreadful death.
Worthy invention
Of immortal minds, ultimate
Of all evils, the gods devised
Old age, where desire
Remains intact, but hope extinct,
The springs of pleasure dry, pain
Ever greater, and good no longer granted.

Little hills and shores, from you
Has gone the glory of the West
That silvered o'er the veil of night,
But you will not long remain
Bereft; from the other side
You will soon see the sky
Whiten anew, and the dawn arise;

Alla qual poscia seguitando il sole,
E folgorando intorno
Con sue fiamme possenti,
Di lucidi torrenti
Inonderà con voi gli eterei campi.
Ma la vita mortal, poi che la bella
Giovinezza sparì, non si colora
D'altra luce giammai, né d'altra aurora.
Vedova è insino al fine; ed alla notte
Che l'altre etadi oscura,
Segno poser gli Dei la sepoltura.

LA GINESTRA

O IL FIORE DEL DESERTO

*E gli uomini vollero piuttosto le tenebre
che la luce.*   Giovanni, III, 19

Qui su l'arida schiena
Del formidabil monte
Sterminator Vesevo,
La qual null'altro allegra arbor né fiore,
Tuoi cespi solitari intorno spargi,
Odorata ginestra,
Contena dei deserti. Anco ti vidi
De' tuoi steli abbellir l'erme contrade
Che cingon la cittade
La qual fu donna de' mortali un tempo,
E del perduto impero
Par che col grave e taciturno aspetto
Faccian fede e ricordo al passeggero.
Or ti riveggo in questo suol, di tristi
Lochi e dal mondo abbandonati amante,

Following after this the sun,
Flashing around
His might beams,
Will flood with shining
Torrents the ethereal fields and you.
But mortal life, once fair
Youth has vanished, is never
Tinged with other light or other dawn.
A widow to the end; and to seal the night
That darkens this other stage,
The gods have set the grave.

MURIEL KITTEL

THE BROOM

OR THE DESERT FLOWER

*And men loved darkness rather than
light.*   John III, 19

Here on the barren spine
Of the stupendous mountain,
That destructor, Vesuvius,
Which takes joy from no other tree or flower,
You scatter tufts of loneliness around,
Sweet-smelling broom,
Patient in the wastelands. As indeed I saw you
Where your stems added beauty to the solitude
Of the dead tracts that brood
Round Rome: that she was queen of cities once,
Set in an empire gone,
Your stalks with their grave silent presence seemed
To witness to the traveller, out of oblivion.
Now I see you again upon this ground,
Lover of sad unpeopled places, unfailing

E d'afflitte fortune ognor compagna.
Questi campi cosparsi
Di ceneri infeconde, e ricoperti
Dell'impietrata lava,
Che sotto i passi al peregrin risona;
Dove s'annida e si contorce al sole
La serpe, e dove al noto
Cavernoso covil torna il coniglio;
Fur liete ville e colti,
E biondeggiàr di spiche, e risonaro
Di muggito d'armenti;
Fur giardini e palagi,
Agli ozi de' potenti
Gradito ospizio; e fur città famose,
Che coi torrenti suoi l'altero monte
Dall'ignea bocca fulminando oppresse
Con gli abitanti insieme. Or tutto intorno
Una ruina involve,
Dove tu siedi, o fior gentile, e quasi
I danni altrui commiserando, al cielo
Di dolcissimo odor mandi un profumo,
Che il deserto consola. A queste piagge
Venga colui che d'esaltar con lode
Il nostro stato ha in uso, e vegga quanto
È il gener nostro in cura
All'amante natura. E la possanza
Qui con giusta misura
Anco estimar potrà dell'uman seme,
Cui la dura nutrice, ov'ei men teme,
Con lieve moto in un momento annulla
In parte, a può con moti
Poco men lievi ancor subitamente
Annichilare in tutto.
Dipinte in queste rive

Comforter of fortunes overthrown.
These fields that are strewn
With unbreeding ashes, sealed down with lava
Turned hard as stone
And echoing to each visiting foot:
Where the snake hides and wriggles, snug in the sun,
And where the rabbit returns
To its well-trodden warren underground:
The plough, and villas, and laughter
Were here once, and the yellowing grain, and music
Of the deep lowing herds;
And gardens and great mansions,
Retreats, establishments
For stately leisure; and those famous cities
Which the insolent mountain from its mouth of fire
Roared down on, struck like lightning, crushed
With all their people. Now one desolation
Transfixes everything,
And in it you sit, gentle flower, as if
Commiserating others' grief, and send
Upwards a breath so very dearly sweet
It must console the desert wastes. These slopes
Should be seen by any man who loves to praise
And exalt our human state: let him see here
How much of human kind
Stands in the care of loving nature. Here also
He can exactly find
The measure of man's living power, a force
In instant jeopardy to his hard nurse,
The earth that with the lightest tremor cancels
A part of it, and with
Others hardly less light can suddenly always
Annihilate it all.
These are excellent slopes

Son dell'umana gente
Le magnifiche sorti e progressive.

Qui mira e qui ti specchia,
Secol superbo e sciocco,
Che il calle insino allora
Dal risorto pensier segnato innanti
Abbandonasti, e volti addietro i passi,
Del ritornar ti vanti,
E procedere il chiami.
Al tuo pargoleggiar gl'ingegni tutti,
Di cui lor sorte rea padre ti fece,
Vanno adulando, ancora
Ch'a ludibrio talora
T'abbian fre sé. Non io
Con tal vergogna scenderò sotterra;
Ma il disprezzo piuttosto che si serra
Di te nel petto mio,
Mostrato avrò quanto si possa aperto:
Ben ch'io sappia che obblio
Preme chi troppo all'età propria increbbe.
Di questo mal, che teco
Mi fia comune, assai finor mi rido.
Libertà vai sognando, e servo a un tempo
Vuoi di novo il pensiero,
Sol per cui risorgemmo
Dalla barbarie in parte, e per cui solo
Si cresce in civiltà, che sola in meglio
Guida i pubblici fati.
Così ti spiacque il vero
Dell'aspra sorte e del depresso loco
Che natura ci diè. Per questo il tergo
Vigliaccamente rivolgesti al lume
Che il fe' palese: e, fuggitivo, appelli
Vil chi lui segue, e solo

For viewing the human soul
With its 'grand destinies and progressive hopes'.

Here, here see your face,
Century of empty pride,
Abandoner of the path
Renascence thought marked forward to our days,
Turning your steps into the past again,
Giving the retreat your praise,
Calling your failure advance!
Your prattling voice has drawn the brilliant, born
Under your bad star, to flatter you
As father, though they mock
You sometimes as they talk
Behind your back. But I
Shall not go down to the grave with shame like theirs;
I hope I can still release the scorn that flares
For you in my heart, and try
To make it felt—or some of it although
I know how history
Crowds out those who over-offend their age.
Well, that is an evil
I must share with you; I have laughed at it before.
Liberty is your great dream, yet you'd make thought
An era's slave again—
Thought, which was our only
Tentative step out of chaos, which alone
Moves us to culture and manners, best, sole
Guide of our general fate!
It seems that the lot of men
Was harsh, the truth displeased you, the narrow place
Which nature gave us. Therefore you miserably
Turned your back upon the light that made
It clear: and you run from that light, calling
Its followers cowards, and only

Magnanimo colui
Che sé schernendo o gli altri, astuto o folle,
Fin sopra gli astri il mortal grado estolle.

Uom di povero stato e membra inferme
Che sia dell'alma generoso ed alto,
Non chiama sé né stima
Ricco d'or né gagliardo,
E di splendida vita o di valente
Persona infra la gente
Non fa risibil mostra;
Ma sé di forza e di tesor mendico
Lascia parer senza vergogna, e noma
Parlando, apertamente, e di sue cose
Fa stima al vero uguale.
Magnanimo animale
Non credo io già, ma stolto,
Quel che nato a perir, nutrito in pene,
Dice, a goder son fatto,
E di fetido orgoglio
Empie le carte, eccelsi fati e nove
Felicità, quali il ciel tutto ignora,
Non pur quest'orbe, promettendo in terra
A popoli che un'onda
Di mar commosso, un fiato
D'aura maligna, un sotterraneo crollo
Distrugge sì che avanza
A gran pena di lor la rimembranza.
Nobil natura è quella
Che a sollevar s'ardisce
Gli occhi mortali incontra
Al comun fato, e che con franca lingua,
Nulla al ver detraendo,
Confessa il mal che ci fu dato in sorte,
E il basso stato e frale;

Those who are foolish or clever
In mocking themselves or others and can extol
The human condition above the stars have 'soul'!

A man who lives poor and in poor health
Yet is well-thinking and generous of spirit
Will call and count himself
Neither wealthy nor hardy,
Nor does he put on a ridiculous show
Of setting up as beau
Or being a prince of men,
But rather lets his state appear, not shamed
By penury of strength or savings, speaks
Openly of what he is, rates what he has
At its unflattered price.
And so the higher flights
Of faith in the greatness of man I decline as witless:
A creature born to perish, schooled by hardships,
Saying 'I was made for happiness,'
Filling volume on volume
With the stench of his boasting, his earthly promises
Of new high destinies and pleasures known
Neither on this globe nor in the whole of heaven—
And this to people whom
A wave of the disturbed sea,
A puff of malignant wind, a shift of the crust
Destroys so thoroughly
That later ages wonder where they lie!
It is a noble nature
That ventures to look up
Through mortal eyes upon
Our common fate, and tell with a frank tongue
That hides no grain of truth
How frailties, evils, low estate are ours
By reason of being born:

Quella che grande e forte
Mostra sé nel soffrir, né gli odii e l'ire
Fraterne, ancor più gravi
D'ogni altro danno, accresce
Alle miserie sue, l'uomo incolpando
Del suo dolor, ma dà la colpa a quella
Che veramente è rea, che de' mortali
Madre è di parto e di voler matrigna.
Costei chiama inimica; e incontro a questa
Congiunta esser pensando,
Siccome è il vero, ed ordinata in pria
L'umana compagnia,
Tutti fra sé confederati estima
Gli uomini, e tutti abbraccia
Con vero amor, porgendo
Valida e pronta ed aspettando aita
Negli alterni perigli e nelle angosce
Della guerra comune. Ed alle offese
Dell'uom armar la destra, e laccio porre
Al vicino ed inciampo,
Stolto crede così qual fora in campo
Cinto d'oste contraria, in sul più vivo
Incalzar degli assalti,
Gl'inimici obbliando, acerbe gare
Imprender con gli amici,
E sparger fuga e fulminar col brando
Infra i propri guerrieri.
Così fatti pensieri
Quando fien, come fur, palesi al volgo,
E quell'orror che primo
Contro l'empia natura
Strinse i mortali in social catena,
Fia ricondotto in parte
Da verace saper, l'onesto e il retto
Conversar cittadino,

One who reveals his strength
And greatness in suffering, refusing to add to
The angers and hates of his brothers
(Worst harm of all within
Our human miseries!) but rather transferring
The blame of grief from man and placing it
In the true seat of guilt, the mother of men
With the stepmother heart. She is the one
He calls his enemy! And since he believes
The brotherhood of men
To be, as indeed they are, united and set
Against this enemy yet,
He takes all men to be confederates
Among themselves, embraces
Them all with a true love,
Extends and expects a ready, meaningful help
As agonies and hazards strike and pass
In the common war of man. And to be armed
Offensively against one's kind, to strew
A neighbor's path with spike
And block he sees as utter madness—like
A man hard pressed upon the battlefield
Who at the crucial assault
Forgets his enemies and begins a sharp
Contest with his own friends,
Spreading the panic of a whistling blade
That cuts its own troops down.
When thoughts like these are known
To ordinary folk, as once they were,
And when that terror which first
Drew mortal men so close
In social links against unpitying nature
Has been won back in part
By true recognition, then will justice, mercy,
Fair and honorable dealing

E giustizia e pietade, altra radice
Avranno allor che non superbe fole,
Ove fondata probità del volgo
Così star suole in piede
Quale star può quel ch'ha in error la sede.

Sovente in queste rive,
Che, desolate, a bruno
Veste il flutto indurato, e par che ondeggi,
Seggo la notte; e su la mesta landa
In purissimo azzuro
Veggo dall'alto fiammeggiar le stelle,
Cui di lontan fa specchio
Il mare, e tutto di scintille in giro
Per lo vòto seren brillare il mondo.
E poi che gli occhi a quelle luci appunto,
Ch'a lor sembrano un punto,
E sono immense, in guisa
Che un punto a petto a lor son terra e mare
Veracemente; a cui
L'uomo non pur, ma questo
Globo ove l'uomo è nulla,
Sconosciuto è del tutto; e quando miro
Quegli ancor più senz'alcun fin remoti
Nodi quasi di stelle,
Ch'a noi paion qual nebbia, a cui non l'uomo
E non la terra sol, ma tutte in uno,
Del numero infinite e della mole,
Con l'aureo sole insiem, le nostre stelle
O sono ignote, o così paion come
Essi alla terra, un punto
Di luce nebulosa; al pensier mio
Che sembri allor, o prole
Dell'uomo? E rimembrando
Il tuo stato quaggiù, di cui fa segno

In the dialogue of cities, find another root
Than the presumptuous idle fables which
Have had to prop the common probity
Of men—if one can call
Error a prop of what is bound to fall.

I often sit at night
Upon these desolate slopes:
Draped in the dark and solid fall of lava
They seem rippling still; and above the joyless
Waste, in purest blue,
I watch the far-off flashing of the stars
Whose fires are mirrored in
The sea, and the whole world is shimmering
With sparks that circle through the empty spaces.
And when I fix my eyes upon these lights,
Mere points to human sight
Yet truly so immense
That all this land and sea in fact is but
A point to them: to them
Not only man but this globe
Where man himself is nothing
Is utterly unknown; and when I see
Still farther off in boundless distances
What looks like knots of stars
Shining to us like mist, and think that to them
Not only man, not only earth, but the whole
System of our stars infinite in number
And mass, together with our own gold sun,
Is either unknown or must appear as they do
To the earth, a point, a node
Of nebular light: how then do you appear
As I sit thinking there,
O seed of man? And recalling
Your poor and worldly state which the mere soil

Il suol ch'io premo; e poi dall'altra parte,
Che te signora e fine
Credi tu data al Tutto, e quante volte
Favoleggiar ti piacque, in questo oscuro
Granel di sabbia, il qual di terra ha nome,
Per tua cagion, dell'universe cose
Scender gli autori, e conversar sovente
Co' tuoi piacevolmente; e che i derisi
Sogni rinnovellando, ai saggi insulta
Fin la presente età, che in conoscenza
Ed in civil costume
Sembra tutte avanzar; qual moto allora,
Mortal prole infelice, o qual pensiero
Verso te finalmente il cor m'assale?
Non so se il riso o la pietà prevale?

Come d'arbor cadeno un picciol pomo,
Cui là nel tardo autunno
Maturità senz'altra forza atterra,
D'un popol di formiche i dolci alberghi,
Cavati in molle gleba
Con gran lavoro, e l'opre
E le ricchezze ch'adunate a prova
Con lungo affaticar l'assidua gente
Avea provvidamente al tempo estivo,
Schiaccia, diserta e copre
In un punto; così d'alto piombando,
Dall'utero tonante
Scagliata al ceil profondo,
Di ceneri e di pomici e di sassi
Notte e ruina, infusa
Di bollenti ruscelli,
O pel montano fianco
Furiosa tra l'erba
Di liquefatti massi

I press on testifies: and then again
Your own belief that you crown
All things with mastery, finality,
And what a favorite tale you cherish still,
How the creators of the cosmic scene
Came down onto this murky grain of sand
Called earth, on your behalf, and often held
Sweet talk with you: and when I see these myths
In their absurdity refurbished to insult
Wise men even today, in an epoch
That seems ahead of all
In knowledge and in culture: what feeling then,
O luckless seed of man, what thought for you
Knocks on my heart when all is said? Laughter?
Pity? Which comes first and which comes after?

A little apple drops down from its tree,
Pulled to the natural earth
By simple ripeness in late autumn days,
And cruches at a single stroke, lays waste
And buries the trim colony
Of ants whose homes were hollowed
Out of that yielding clay
With such hard labor to them, their works and wealth
Amassed with long exertions all that summer,
Trials of diligence followed
By a provident folk: so also, plummeting down,
Hurled from a thundering womb
Up to the fathomless sky,
A night and ruin of rocks
And ash and pumice mingled
With boiling streams, or the vast
Torrent of metals and molten
Boulders and sizzling sand
Falling along the hill-flank,

E di metalli e d'infocata arena
Scendendo immensa piena,
Le cittadi che il mar là su l'estremo
Lido aspergea, confuse
E infranse e ricoperse
In pochi istanti: onde su quelle or pasce
La capra, e città nove
Sorgon dall'altra banda, a cui sgabello
Son le sepolte, e le prostrate mura
L'arduo monte al suo piè quasi calpesta.
Non ha natura al seme
Dell'uom più stima o cura
Che alla formica: e se più rara in quello
Che nell'altra è la strage,
Non avvien ciò d'altronde
Fuor che l'uom sue prosapie ha men feconde.

Ben mille ed ottocento
Anni varcàr poi che spariro, oppressi
Dall'ignea forza, i popolati seggi,
E il villanello intento
Ai vigneti, che a stento in questi campi
Nutre la morta zolla e incenerita,
Ancor leva lo sguardo
Sospettoso alla vetta
Fatal, che nulla mai fatta più mite
Ancor siede tremenda, ancor minaccia
A lui strage ed ai figli ed agli averi
Lor poverelli. E spesso
Il meschino in sul tetto
Dell'ostel villereccio, alla vagante
Aura giacendo tutta notte insonne,
E balzando più volte, esplora il corso
Del temuto bollor, che si riversa
Dall'inesausto grembo

Raging down unrepulsed
Through the grass, smashed and convulsed
And covered over in a few moments of time
These cities which the sea
Washed at the edge of the shore:
And now above the cities the goat browses,
And on the other slope
New cities rise, they stand upon the stool
Of the entombed ones and the prostrate walls
The bitter mountain seems to tramp to dust.
Nature has no more care
Or praise for human souls
Than for the ants: and if she slaughters men
Less terribly than them,
This is no great wonder,
For man's fecundity and ants' are worlds asunder.

Eighteen hundred years
And more have passed since those great populated
Places vanished, crushed by the power of fire,
And still the peasant's fears,
As he watches his vines struggle in these fields
To nourish life on sterile cindery clods,
Cause him to keep one eye
Warily on the fatal peak
Which never yet was moved to become gentle
But still sits awe-inspiring there, still threatens
Destruction to him and his children and their
Pitiful handful of possessions.
And often the wretched man
Stretched on the rustic roof
Of his home, lying there all night sleepless
In the wandering breeze, and time and again
Jumping to his feet, gazes along the course
Of the dreaded flux which waits to boil and pour

Su l'arenoso dorso, a cui riluce
Di Capri la marina
E di Napoli il porto e Mergellina.
E se appressar lo vede o se nei cupo
Del domestico pozzo ode mai l'acqua
Fervendo gorgogliar, desta i figliuoli,
Desta la moglie in fretta, e via, con quanto
Di lor cose rapir posson, fuggendo,
Vede lontan l'usato
Suo nido, e il picciol campo,
Che gli fu dalla fame unico schermo,
Preda al flutto rovente,
Che crepitando giunge, e inesorato
Durabilmente sovra quei si spiega.
Torna al celeste raggio
Dopo l'antica obblivion l'estinta
Pompei, come sepolto
Scheletro, cui di terra
Avarizia o pietà rende all'aperto;
E al deserto foro
Diritto infra le file
Dei mozzi colonnati il peregrino
Lunge contempla il bipartito giogo
E la cresta fumante,
Che alla sparsa ruina ancor minaccia.
E nell'orror della secreta notte
Per li vacui teatri,
Per li templi deformi e per le rotte
Case, ove i parti il pipistrello asconde,
Come sinistra face
Che per vòti palagi atra s'aggiri,
Corre il baglior della funerea lava,
Che di lontan per l'ombre
Rosseggia e i lochi intorno intorno tinge.
Così, dell'uomo ignara e dell'etadi

From unimpoverished cells
Along that gritty crest and raise its glow
On Margellina and
The port of Naples, on Capri and its sand.
And if he sees it coming down, or if
He ever hears a gurgling ferment in
The depths of his garden well, he hurriedly
Wakens his children, rouses his wife, and runs
With them, taking what things they can, far off
Till looking back he sees
His nest and home, his field—
His tiny, only shield against starvation—
Caught by the red-hot flood
Which crackles as it comes and over these
Victims settles, relentless, without appeal.
After long forgetfulness
Extinct Pompeii returns to daylight like
A buried skeleton
Brought out into the air
By worldly greed or pity; and the traveller,
Paused in the empty forum,
Looks through the stricken rows
Of colonnades and gazes with intentness
Up to the mass of the divided summit
With its smoking crater-ridge
Still menacing the ruins scattered there.
And in the secrecy and horror of the dark
Through vacant theatres,
Through mutilated temples and through stark
Shells of houses where bats hide their young,
The glow of the deadly lava
Like terror wandering with a sinister
Torch through empty palaces, runs on
And reddens in the shadows
Of the distance and paints every place it meets.

Ch'ei chiama antiche, e del seguir che fanno
Dopo gli avi i nepoti,
Sta natura ognor verde, anzi procede
Per sì lungo cammino
Che sembra star. Caggiono i regni intanto,
Passan genti e linguaggi: ella nol vede:
E l'uom d'eternità s'arroga il vanto.

E tu, lenta ginestra,
Che di selve odorate
Queste campagne dispogliate adorni,
Anche tu presto alla crudel possanza
Soccomberai del sotterraneo foco,
Che ritornando al loco
Già noto, stenderà l'avaro lembo
Su tue molli foreste. E piegherai
Sotto il fascio mortal non renitente
Il tuo capo innocente:
Ma non piegato insino allora indarno
Codardamente supplicando innanzi
Al futuro oppressor; ma non eretto
Con forsennato orgoglio inver le stelle,
Né sul deserto, dove
E la sede e i natali
Non per voler ma per fortuna avesti;
Ma più saggia, ma tanto
Meno inferma dell'uom, quanto le frali
Tue stirpi con credesti
O dal fato o da te fatte immortali.

So nature, unaware of man and eras
Man calls ancient, unaware of links
From ancestors to sons,
Stands always green, or rather sets her feet
On such a lengthy road
She seems to stand. Meanwhile kingdoms decay,
Peoples and tongues die out: she does not see it:
And man presumes on his eternity.

And you, yielding broom,
Decking these ravaged fields
With your sweet-smelling groves, you too
Will soon go down before the cruel fires
Of that great subterranean dominion:
They will return to their station
As before, their hungry hems will crawl
Over your soft thickets. And you will bend
Your innocent head with unreluctant nod
Under that deadly load:
But not a head you bent till then in vain
With cowardly entreaty praying for
Your future killer's grace: not lifted up
In frantic vanity towards the stars,
Or over this wasteland where
Your birth and growing-place
Were yours not by your choice but that of fate:
But wiser and less weak,
So much less weak than man, since you could rate
Your truly fragile race
With no self-won, no destined deathless state.

EDWIN MORGAN

II

Operette Morali

THE HISTORY OF MANKIND

[STORIA DEL GENERE UMANO]

It is said that all the men who peopled the earth in the begin-
ning were created everywhere simultaneously, and all as in-
fants; that they were nurtured by bees, goats, and doves, ex-
actly as the poets fabled about the rearing of Jove. The earth
was much smaller than it is now, the land almost all flat, the
sky without stars, and the sea uncreated. Altogether there ap-
peared much less variety and splendor in the world than is
seen now. Nevertheless, men took an inexhaustible delight in
observing and examining heaven and earth, marveling at them
exceedingly. They thought them very beautiful, and not
merely vast but of infinite extent and majesty and loveliness.
Moreover, because they sustained themselves on the most joy-
ful expectations and drew incredible pleasure from each one
of the sensations of their lives, they grew up very contented,
and believed themselves to be almost completely happy. But
after spending their childhood and early youth in this way,
and reaching a maturer age, they began to experience certain
transformations. It seemed to them that the expectations
whose fulfillment they had until then gone on deferring from
day to day, since they continued to lead to nothing, deserved
little trust. Yet it appeared to them impossible to content
themselves with what they could enjoy in the present without
anticipating any increase in well-being. This was particularly
so because the appearance of natural things and each aspect
of daily life did not turn out to be as delightful and gratifying
to them finally as they were in the beginning, either through
habituation or because of a lessening of the mind's original
vivacity. They wandered about the earth visiting the most re-
mote regions, which they could easily do because the country
was flat, and neither divided by seas nor obstructed by other

difficulties. So that not many years passed before most of them noticed that the earth, though large, had definite limits which were not so vast as to be unencompassable, and that, except for very slight differences, all the parts of the earth and all its inhabitants were very similar one to another. Wherefore their discontent so increased that they were not yet past their youth when a distaste for their own existence became universal among them. By degrees during manhood and increasingly in their declining years, when satiety became loathing, some of them reached such a pitch of despair that they gave up of their own accord, some in one way, some another, the light and life they in their early years had so much loved and were now unable to bear.

To the Gods it seemed horrifying that living creatures should prefer death to life and that, unforced by necessity or any other contributing circumstance, life itself should become the instrument of its own undoing in any one of its creatures. Nor is it easy to convey how much they marveled that their gifts should be considered so vile and loathsome as to cause others to do all in their power to give them up and reject them. For they thought they had set in the world so much bounty and delight, such provision and order that it was made into an abode not merely to be endured but to be loved by every animal and particularly by man, a species they had made with unique care into a marvel of excellence. Though they were touched with no little compassion for all the human misery made clear by the event, still, they also feared lest the repetition and multiplication of those grim examples should shortly cause the human race to perish, contrary to the decrees of fate, and thus deprive creation of the perfection accrued to it by our race, and themselves of those honors they received from mankind.

Jove found it advisable, therefore, to improve the human condition and to give it greater means of happiness. Men, he understood, complained principally that things were neither immeasurably big nor infinitely beautiful, perfect, and various, as they originally thought, but instead were limited, imperfect, and uniform. They longed for the sweetness of their early years and fervently prayed to be returned to childhood and continue in it all their lives, lamenting not only their old age but maturity and even youth itself. However, Jove could not satisfy this longing in them, since it was contrary to the universal laws of nature and to the functions and purposes which the divine intention and decrees meant men to exercise and fulfill. Neither could he share his own infinity with mortal creatures, nor make matter infinite, nor give infinite perfection to things and infinite happiness to men. Nonetheless, it did seem to him proper to extend the limits of creation and to adorn and diversify it further. With this intent, he enlarged the earth on every side and poured in the sea between the inhabited places so as to vary the appearance of things by cutting off the roads, thus preventing the limits from being easily discovered by men, while at the same time suggesting to men's eyes a living semblance of immensity. Then it was that the new waters took possession of the continent of Atlantis, and not of it alone but countless other very extensive tracts, though of it there remains only the particular memory surviving the multitude of centuries. Many places he depressed, many he raised up, bringing forth the mountains and the hills; and he strewed the night with stars. He refined and purified the quality of the air and increased the clearness and light of day. He intensified the colors of the sky and of the landscape and blended them with greater variety than before. He mingled the generations of men, making the old age of some coincide with the youth and boyhood of others. He decided that, since he could not satisfy them with the reality, he would multiply the semblances of infinity, which men desired above everything else. And since it was, as he understood it, to the virtue of imagination that they chiefly owed the very great bliss of their childhood, he wished to foster and nourish it. Along with the other expedients he had put into operation for that purpose, such as the sea, he now created echo and hid it in the valleys and caverns, and in the forests he set a hoarse and profound clamor and a vast undulation of the trees. He also created the brood of dreams and charged them with making visible to men, through different forms of illusion, that plenitude of incomprehensible happiness which even he could not create, and those intricate and undefinable fantasies, any real counterparts of which he himself could not have produced even though he wanted to and though men ardently yearned for them.

So then, through these provisions of Jove, man's spirit was restored and uplifted, and in each was renewed pleasure and love of life, as well as appreciation, delight, and astonishment at the beauty and immensity of terrestrial things. And this happy state lasted longer than the first, chiefly because of the intervals of time introduced by Jove in the matter of births, so that spirits chilled and wearied by experience were comforted by the sight of the warmth and hopefulness of green youth. But in process of time, when the novelty again seemed quite gone, tedium and disdain of life revived and reasserted themselves, and men were reduced to a state of dejection. Then, it is believed, was originated the custom recorded in histories as practiced by certain ancient peoples—that when anyone was born, his relatives and their friends would gather to mourn him; and when he died, that day would be celebrated with festivities and orations congratulating the deceased. Finally all mortals turned towards impiety, either because they thought they were not listened to by Jove or because it is the very nature of misery to harden and corrupt even the noblest spirits and alienate them from honor and righteousness. They are entirely wrong therefore who think that human unhappiness was originally born of iniquity and acts committed against the Gods; rather, on the contrary, from their calamities did the wickedness of men stem, and not otherwise.

Now after the arrogance of mortals was punished by the

Gods with the flood of Deucalion and vengeance for their of-
fences had been taken, Deucalion and Pyrrha, the two sole
survivors of that universal disaster of our kind, acknowledg-
ing to themselves that nothing could be of greater benefit to
the human race than complete extinction, sat on the summit of
a crag calling on death with irresistible longing, so little did
they fear or lament the common lot. Nonetheless, being ad-
monished by Jove to remedy the desolation of the earth and
finding it unbearable to begin the work of generation, discon-
solate and contemptuous of life as they were, they took stones
from the mountains, as the Gods showed them, and casting
them over their shoulders they re-established the human spe-
cies. But what had passed had made Jove aware of the true na-
ture of men; that it cannot suffice them, like the other animals,
to live and be free of every physical pain and discomfort;
rather that always and in whatever condition they crave the
impossible, and the less they are afflicted by other evils the
more they of their own accord torment themselves with this
longing of theirs. He decided therefore to avail himself of new
expedients for preserving this miserable species, and these
were principally two. One was to mix true evils with their
lives, the other to involve them in a thousand activities and la-
bors, with the sole purpose of occupying men and distracting
them as much as possible from preoccupation with themselves,
or at least with that longing of theirs for inconceivable and im-
possible happiness.

Thus he first spread among them a multitude of different
diseases and an infinite variety of other misfortunes; partly
because he wanted to forestall satiety by varying the condi-
tions and the fortunes of mortal life and, by contrast with the
evils, to increase the value of their blessings; partly so that
the shortage of pleasures should, to beings accustomed to
worse things, prove much more bearable than it had in the
past; and partly also with the intention of breaking and tam-
ing the wildness of men, of training them to bow their heads

and yield to necessity, of bringing them to the point where they could more easily be satisfied with their lot, and of blunting the keenness and vehemence of longing in spirits enfeebled by bodily infirmities no less than by their own distresses. Besides, he knew it would happen that men weighed down by diseases and calamities would be less prompt than in the past to turn their hands against themselves, because they would be cowed and their spirit prostrate, which results from habituation to sufferings. And these sufferings, giving place as they do to the greatest hopes, are also wont to bind men's spirits to life: for the unhappy have the firm conviction that they might be most happy, if only they could recover from their misfortunes, which, as is the nature of man, they never cease trusting will somehow happen to them. Next he created tempests of wind and storm-clouds, armed himself with thunder and lightning, gave Neptune the trident, sent comets whirling about, and ordained eclipses. By these means, along with other terrifying portents and phenomena, he decided to frighten mortals from time to time, knowing that fear and the presence of danger would reconcile not only the unhappy to life, at least briefly, but even those who would be more bent on fleeing it because they held it in greater abhorrence.

And to preclude their former indolence, he instilled in the human race a need and appetite for novel kinds of food and drink which they could provide for themselves only with great and difficult labor. For men quenched their thirst only with water until the time of the flood, and fed on herbs and fruits which the earth and the trees ministered to them naturally, and on other nourishment crude and easy to procure, such as some peoples, the California Indians in particular, use to sustain themselves even to this day. To different places he assigned different celestial qualities and varied likewise the portions of the year, which up to that time had been, invariably and in all the earth, so benign and pleasant that men had not had any use for clothing. They were, however, forced from then on to provide it for themselves and with great industriousness to counteract the changes and inclemencies of the weather. He commanded Mercury to found the first cities; to divide the human race by peoples, nations, and tongues, thus setting rivalry and discord among them; and to acquaint men with song and those other arts which because of both their nature and origin were and continue to be called divine. He himself established laws, states, and civil constitutions among the new peoples. And finally, wanting to favor them with an incomparable gift, he sent among them certain idols of a most exalted-seeming and superhuman appearance, to whom, in large part, he allowed direction and power over these people: they were called Justice, Virtue, Glory, Patriotism, and other such names. Among them there was also one called Love, who like the others then first came to earth. For before the use of clothing not love but a carnal impulse, not dissimilar in men at the time from what it has always been in the brutes, drove one sex towards the other in the same way that everyone is drawn towards food and similar things, which are not truly loved but craved.

It was remarkable how much fruit these divine decisions bore for mortal life and, notwithstanding the toils, the fears, the sufferings—things previously unknown to our kind—how much the new conditions of men surpassed, in comfort and pleasantness, those that had existed before the flood. Indeed, to a great extent this effect was produced by those marvelous apparitions who were reputed by men to be either genii or deities, and whom, for a very long period of time, men followed and worshipped with inestimable ardor and with immense and astonishing labor, fired to it with boundless energy on the part of poets and illustrious artists; so much so that a very great number of mortals did not hesitate to offer up and sacrifice their blood and their very lives, some to one, some to another of those idols. Which was far from displeasing to

Jove, rather it pleased him exceedingly, because along with other considerations, he also thought that men would feel much less free to throw away their lives voluntarily the more ready they were to expend them on worthy and glorious causes. These salutary institutions greatly surpassed the preceding ones, even in duration. Indeed, by virtue of them human life had been, for a certain period in particular, almost joyful. And although after many centuries they fell into apparent decadence, nevertheless, even while declining and failing, they were so effective that until the beginning of an age not far removed from the present one, life remained moderately easy and bearable, thanks to them.

The grounds and mode of their deterioration were as follows: the many ingenious devices discovered by men in order to provide easily and quickly for their particular needs; the excessive increase in the original inequalities of circumstance and station instituted by Jove among men when he founded and ordered the first commonwealths; the indolence and futility which for those very reasons, after ancient banishment, once again seized life; the fact that in life, not only in actuality but also in men's estimation, the appeal of variety had lessened, as always happens with long familiarity; and then other graver matters which, because many have already described and made them known, need not be specified. Clearly there was renewed in men that tedium with their affairs which had distressed them before the flood, and there was refreshed that bitter longing for a happiness unknown and alien to the nature of the universe.

But the complete reversal of their fortune and the final issue of that phase which we now usually call antiquity, came mainly from one cause different from those already mentioned, and it was this. Among the apparitions so esteemed by the ancients there was one called in their language Wisdom, who, universally honored, like all her companions, and particularly followed by many, had contributed her share to the well-being of past centuries equally with the others. Time and again, daily indeed, she promised and vowed to her followers that she would show them Truth, a great spirit and her own master, who had never come down on earth but sat with the Gods in heaven, and whom she promised, of her own authority and grace, she would draw down and induce to wander among men for some length of time. Through that association and familiarity, mankind was bound to reach such a level that in depth of knowledge, in excellence of institutions and customs, and in happiness it would become comparable almost with the divine. But how could a mere shadow and empty appearance carry promises into effect, let alone bring Truth down to earth? After very long belief and trust in them, men came to see the vanity of those promises. At the same time they were famished for novelty, particularly because of the slothfulness with which they lived. Partly stimulated also by their ambition to be equal to the Gods, and partly by the desire for that felicity which from the words of the idol they supposed themselves to be about to attain by contact with Truth; they turned to Jove and in the most insistent and presumptuous voices demanded that he grant earth for a certain period of time the presence of that most noble spirit: charging that he was depriving his creatures of the infinite benefit they would derive from her presence. And along with this they complained to him about the human lot, renewing their old and offensive complaints against the meanness and poverty of things. For those enticing apparitions, the source of so much good to past ages, were by most now held in little esteem, not that they already knew them for what they truly were, but that the common meanness of thought and slackness of custom was such that almost no one followed them any longer. Therefore men cried out, wickedly cursing the greatest gift that the eternal Gods had made or could have made to mortals, that the earth was graced by none but the lesser spirits, while it was not thought becoming or permissible for the great ones, to whom the human race might more fittingly bow, to set foot on this lowliest portion of the universe.

Many things had long since renewed the alienation of the will of Jove from men, and among others the unparalleled vices and misdeeds which in number and grievousness left far behind the wickedness avenged by the flood. Human nature sickened him wholly after so much experience with it; restless, insatiable, immoderate human nature, whose tranquility, let alone happiness, he now felt certain that no provision would bring about, no condition satisfy, no place suffice. Even if he had wanted to add a thousandfold to the spaciousness and pleasures of the earth and to the manysided totality of things, to men, as covetous of attaining the infinite as they were incapable, all of this would shortly seem confining, unpleasant, and valueless. And in the end those foolish and arrogant demands so aroused the wrath of the god that putting all pity aside he decided to punish mankind forever, condemning it throughout all future ages to a misery much worse than the past. For that purpose he decided to send Truth to remain among men not for a time merely, as they demanded, but to give her eternal domicile among them and, removing those comely idols whom he had set here below, to make her permanent arbiter and master of human beings.

The other Gods were astonished at this decision; for it appeared to them that it might result in too great an exaltation of our condition and jeopardize their own superiority. From this notion Jove freed them however by demonstrating that, aside from the fact that not all the genii, even the great ones, were in themselves beneficent, the genius of Truth was not such as to have the same effects on men as on the Gods. While to the immortals she made evident their beatitude, to men she would fully disclose their own unhappiness and continually hold it up to them before their very eyes, revealing it besides as not merely the work of fortune, but such that no chance or remedy would enable them to escape it or ever in life find respite from it. And since the greater part of their evils are evils only to the extent that they are believed to be by those who bear them and are more or less grievous according to the way men judge them, you can understand what a great mischief the presence of this spirit will soon become to men. For nothing will appear more profoundly true to them than the falseness of all mortal good, and nothing more substantial than the hollowness of all things other than their own suffering. For these reasons they will be deprived even of hope, thanks to which, more than to any other pleasure or solace, they have endured life, from the beginning until now. Without hope and seeing for their enterprises and labors no worthwhile end in view, they will arrive at such a state of indifference and abhorrence of all active, let alone large-minded effort, that the common ways of the living will little differ from that of the dead. Yet in this state of hopelessness and indolence they will not be able to prevent their inborn desire for boundless happiness from stinging and vexing them even more than in the past, since now they will be less involved and less distracted by variety in their pursuits and by incentive in action. At the same time they will find themselves deprived of their natural power of imagination, which alone could in some measure have realized for them this happiness neither possible nor understood by me nor by those who themselves yearn for it. And all those semblances of infinity which I carefully put into the world in order to delude and sustain them according to their inclination with grand and indefinable thoughts, will have become inadequate and ineffective because of the knowledge and habit of mind they will have acquired from Truth. So that earth and the other parts of the universe, if they seemed small to them in the past, henceforth will seem miniscule, both because men will be instructed and enlightened about the mysteries of nature and because, contrary to their present expectation, the more informed they are, the more confined things will appear to them. Finally, because the idols will have been removed from the earth and the teachings of Truth will have given men full cognizance of the nature of them, human life will lack all valor and integrity of thought and deed. The very names of nations and countries, let alone zeal and love for them, will be extinguished everywhere; and all men will gather, as they will be wont to say, into a single nation and country, as in the beginning, and will profess universal love for all their kind; but in reality the human race will disintegrate into as many peoples as there are men. For having neither a country particularly to love nor foreigners to hate, each one will hate all the rest and love, of his kind, himself only. To relate how many and what inconveniences will result from this would be interminable. But even in such great and desperate unhappiness mortals will not of their own accord dare to quit the light of day, since the sway of this spirit will make them no less cowardly than miserable, and while adding beyond measure to the bitterness of their life, she will deprive them of the courage to reject it.

It seemed to the Gods that our lot, according to Jove's words, was going to be so harsh and terrible, it would not consort with divine compassion to consent to it. But Jove continued, saying: However, they will have some modicum of comfort from that idol they call Love, whom I am disposed, while removing all others, to leave in human company. Nor will it be given Truth, powerful though she is and continually embattled, ever to drive out or, except rarely, to vanquish Love. So that the lives of men engaged equally in the worship of the idol and the spirit, will be split and the two will between them have common sway over the affairs and minds of mortals. In most men all other interests will diminish, except some unimportant few. Those weighed down with age will be compensated for their lack of the consolations of Love by the blessing of their natural disposition to be very nearly content with mere life, as befalls other kinds of animals, and to cherish it diligently for its own sake and not for any pleasure or comfort they may derive from it.

So having removed those blessed idols from the earth, except only Love, the least noble of all, Jove sent Truth to men
and gave her permanent place and mastery among them. From
this ensued all those grievous consequences he had forseen;
for a very astonishing thing occurred. That spirit had, before
her descent, when she had neither power nor right over men,
been honored by them with a huge number of temples and offerings. Now, having come down to earth with regal authority
and having begun to make her presence known, she, in contrast with all other immortals, who the more clearly they reveal themselves the more worthy of veneration they appear,
so aggrieved the minds of men and smote them with such horror that, though forced to obey, they refused to worship her.
And whereas the other apparitions were most revered and
loved by those beings over whom they most exercised their
power, this spirit won the fiercest curses and the deepest
hatred from those over whom she held the greatest sway. But,
nevertheless, being unable either to evade or resist her tyranny,
mortals lived in that supreme misery which up to now they
have endured and always will.

However, compassion, which in celestial minds is never extinguished, moved the will of Jove not long since to pity so
much unhappiness, and to pity especially the unhappiness of
certain men distinguished by fineness of intellect, combined
with nobility of conduct and integrity of life, who were, he
saw, commonly oppressed and afflicted more than any others
by the power and harsh dominance of that spirit. In ancient
times, when Justice, Virtue, and the other idols governed human affairs, it used to be that the Gods sometimes visited their
creatures, now one, now another coming down to earth and
manifesting his presence in various ways; and this had always
brought the greatest benefit either to mortals in general or to

some one in particular. But life having been corrupted anew and sunk entirely in wickedness, the Gods for a very long time disdained human association. Now Jove, pitying our extreme unhappiness, inquired whether any of the immortals might be disposed to visit, as they used to do of old, and to console their progeny in its great travail, those of them particularly who appeared in themselves undeserving of this universal wretchedness. When all the others remained silent, Love, the son of Celestial Venus, corresponding in name to the idol so called, but in his nature, qualities, and effects very different, volunteered (for his compassion is outstanding among the Gods) to undertake the mission indicated by Jove and to descend from heaven, from which he had never before parted. Since the council of the immortals held him so ineffably dear, they did not suffer him to depart from their company even for the shortest time; although, deluded from time to time by the metamorphoses and various other deceptions of the idol of the same name, many of the ancients fancied themselves to have had indubitable signs of the presence of this highest of deities. But he did not begin to visit mortals until they were put under the sway of Truth. And since then he is wont to come down only rarely and to remain briefly, both because of the general unworthiness of human beings and because it is only with the greatest uneasiness that the Gods bear his separation from them. When he comes down to earth, he chooses from among the most generous and great-spirited people the tenderest and gentlest hearts; and there he dwells briefly, diffusing a rare and wonderful serenity and filling them with such noble feelings and with so much virtue and fortitude that they then experience—a thing wholly new for human beings—the reality rather than the semblance of perfect happiness. Only very rarely he joins two hearts together, encompassing both at the same time and instilling mutual ardor and desire, although he is entreated to do so with the greatest urgency by all those whom he possesses. More than some few, however, Jove does not permit him to gratify, because the happiness born of this blessing is such that the divine itself surpasses it by too slight an interval. In any event, to be filled with his divine presence of itself transcends even the most fortunate conditions of any man in the very best of times. Around him on whom he lights whirl invisible to all others those stunning apparitions whom, though now barred from human intimacy, the God brings back on earth for this purpose. Being permitted by Jove, it is not in Truth's power to forbid it, although she is most hostile to those idols and in her innermost being greatly offended by their return: still, it is not, by the very nature of such spirits, given them to withstand the Gods. And since Love is endowed by the fates with eternal youth, consonant with this nature of his, he fulfills in his fashion the earliest entreaty of men: to be returned to the state of childhood. For in the spirit of those he elects to inhabit, he arouses and revives, while he is there, the infinite hope and beautiful and dear fantasies of their tender years. Many mortals, unacquainted with and incapable of his delights, scoff and revile him with unbridled audacity day in and day out, whether in his absence or in his presence. He, however, does not listen to their insults, nor would he exact any punishment for them if he did, so magnanimous and meek is he by nature. Besides, content with the vengeance they exact of the whole human race and with the incurable misery which afflicts it, the immortals do not trouble about the individual offenses of men. Nor are the fraudulent, the unjust, and the contemners of the Gods specially punished in any way, other than simply to remain what they are, and thus be alienated from the divine grace.

GINO L. RIZZO & MILTON MILLER

PRIZES PROPOSED BY THE
ACADEMY OF SATIRISTS

[PROPOSTA DI PREMI FATTA DALL'ACCADEMIA DEI SILLOGRAFI]

The Academy of Satirists, constantly desiring to further as much as possible the public welfare, and convinced that nothing is more conducive to this end than assisting and promoting the movement and inclinations

Of this most fortunate age in which we live . . .

(as an illustrious poet has remarked) has taken into its serious consideration the quality and the image of our time, and after a long and careful investigation has resolved upon the appellation "The Age of Machines," not only because the men of today live and act more mechanically than did those of the past, but also because of the enormous number of machines invented lately and adapted to so many varied functions, that, as a result, one cannot say that men, but instead machines, deal with human activities and accomplish the tasks of life. In relation to the aforesaid, the Academy wishes to express its greatest pleasure, not only for the obvious comforts which are hereby derived, but also for two reasons which it judges to be of the utmost importance, though generally overlooked. The first being that it believes that ultimately the functions and applications of machines must be expanded beyond material things even into the spiritual; wherefore, seeing that by virtue of the aforesaid machines we are now free and secure from injury from lightning and hailstorms and from many other evils of the kind, so from time to time there will be invented, for instance—and the reader is begged to excuse the neologisms—some anti-jealousy device, some anti-calumny, some anti-perfidy, or some anti-fraud machine; some health-rod or some other engine to protect us from egotism, from the predominance of mediocrity, from the prosperity of the stupid and the lewd and the vile, from universal indifference, from the unhappiness of the wise and the polite and the generous, and from other inconveniences which for all these many years we have regarded as unavoidable, as were once the effects of lightning and hailstorms.

The second and more important reason is that since most philosophers despair of ever being able to cure the defects of the human race, declaring them to be much greater and more numerous than its virtues, and deeming it easier to remake it altogether, or to substitute a new species for it, instead of correcting it, therefore the Academy of Satirists believes it to be most expedient that men remove themselves as far as possible from the affairs of life, gradually giving way and allowing the machines to take their places. Thus, having decided to assist in promoting as far as possible the new order of things, it now proposes three prizes for those who shall invent the three machines described hereunder:

1. The first shall be capable of acting as a true friend which will neither mock nor censure its friend when absent; which shall not suffer itself to bear the hearing of its friend's being taken or put to ridicule; which shall not prefer the reputation of being stinging or biting, nor the eliciting of the laughter of men at the risk of losing friendship; which shall not divulge for some ulterior reason or for having material for gossip or for being ostentatious any secret committed to it; which shall not prevail upon the familiarity or the confidence of its friend in order to supplant him or to climb over him more easily; which shall not bear envy against his advantages; which shall take care of its own good and either avoid or make reparation for damages incurred; and which shall be prompt in responding to demands and needs, otherwise than by words.

For the other qualities required in this automaton, the inventor must keep his eye upon the treatises of Cicero and the Marquise de Lambert on friendship. The Academy believes that the invention of such a machine should not be adjudicated impossible, nor in any way excessively difficult. Aside from the automatic devices of Regiomontano, of Vaucanson and others, especially that one in London which designs figures and portraits and writes down whatever is spoken to it, machines have been invented which are capable of playing chess. Now, in the judgment of many wise men, human life is but a game, and some affirm that it is a thing even lighter than chess and, among other considerations, that the form of chess proceeds according to reason and more prudently ordered moves than does the game of life. According to Pindar, life is no more substantial than the shadow of a dream, and hence certainly lies within the capacity of an automaton. As far as speech is concerned, there appears to be no doubt that men have the power to bestow it upon the machines which they create, as is proved by various examples: to wit, from what one reads about the Statue of Memnon and the talking head made by Albertus Magnus, which was so talkative that St. Thomas Aquinas lost patience with it and broke it. And if the parrot of Nevers (despite the fact that that was an animal) knew how to talk and answer when addressed, why should it not be possible for the mind of man to imagine and construct a machine as loquacious as the parrot of Nevers or other birds which we see and hear every day?

The inventor of this machine will receive as prize a gold medal of the weight of four hundred sequins, the one side of which shall show the images of Orestes and Pylades; and the other, the name of the winner, with the following inscription:

FIRST REALIZER OF THE ANCIENT FABLES

2. The second machine should be an artificial steam-man, constructed for the purpose of performing virtuous and generous acts. The Academy believes hot air to be profitable for energizing this self-mover (since no other means seems to be available) and for directing it toward tasks of virtue and glory.

Those who would undertake the invention of such a machine should consult poems and romances, where they may find in operation the qualities and functions with which this automaton should be endowed. The prize will be a gold medal of the weight of four hundred and fifty sequins, stamped on the top with some meaningful suggestion of the Golden Age, and on the reverse the following inscription lifted from the *Fourth Eclogue* of Vergil:

LET IRON CEASE AND FOLK OF GOLD RISE OVER ALL THE EARTH

3. The third machine should be equipped for performing the offices of the ideal woman imagined on the one hand by Count Baldassare Castiglione, who delineated it in his book *The Courtier*, and on the other hand by other writers whose works are readily available and which should be consulted and followed, as even that of the Count. Nor should the invention of such a machine seem impossible to the men of our times, since Pygmalion, in very ancient times far removed from science, was able to manufacture a wife with his own hands, and she is considered the best woman who ever existed. The creator of this machine should receive a gold medal of the weight of five hundred sequins, on which will be depicted on one side the Arabian Phoenix of Metastasio, perched on a plant of European origin, and on the other side will be engraved the name of the winner with the following inscription:

INVENTOR OF FAITHFUL WOMEN AND CONJUGAL BLISS

The Academy has decreed that to meet the expenses incurred for these prizes, they must take what was discovered in the Sack of Diogenes (past Secretary of the Academy) or one of the three golden jackasses which belonged to three other past members: viz., Apuleius, Firenzuola, and Machiavelli; all these things bequeathed to the Academy through the wills of its members, as duly recorded in its transactions.

JAMES WILHELM

DIALOGUE BETWEEN NATURE AND A SOUL
[DIALOGO DELLA NATURA E DI UN'ANIMA]

Nature: Go, my dear daughter, my favorite, for so you will be thought of and such you will be called through a long course of centuries. Live, and be great and unhappy.

Soul: What wrong did I commit before beginning to live that you condemn me to this punisment?

Nature: What punishment, my child?

Soul: Do you not sentence me to be unhappy?

Nature: Only insofar as I want you to be great, and it is impossible to be the one without being the other. Besides, you are destined to animate a human body and all human beings are born and live unhappy by necessity.

Soul: But it would be better for you to condition them to be happy by necessity; or if you cannot, you ought to keep from bringing them into the world.

Nature: Neither one is in my power. Fate, to whom I am subordinate, ordains otherwise, for whatever reason, which neither you nor I can understand. Now that you have been created and formed to animate a human being, no force whatever, neither mine nor any other, has the power to spare you the unhappiness common to men. But beyond that you will also have to endure a much greater unhappiness of your own because of the excellence with which I have endowed you.

Soul: So far I have comprehended nothing at all; having only just now begun to live, this must be the reason why I do not understand you. Tell me though, are excellence and excessive unhappiness substantially the same thing? Of if they are two distinct things, couldn't you separate one from the other?

Nature: In the souls of men and proportionately in that of all species of animals, these two things can be said to be almost the same, because the excellence of their souls implies a higher degree of life in them, and this implies greater sensitivity to their own unhappiness, which is to say, greater unhappiness. Similarly, their greater animation of spirit involves a greater capacity for responding to the appropriate claims of the self, whatever its bent and however it may be manifested. This superior capacity of response to the claims of self carries with it a greater desire for happiness and therefore greater discontent and distress when deprived of it and greater suffering from the adversities that supervene. All this is inherent in the original and permanent order of creation, which I cannot change. Besides this, the fineness of your own intellect and the liveliness of your imagination will cut you off from any large degree of mastery over yourself. The lower animals to attain their purposes make easy use of all their faculties and energies. But men very seldom make use of all their powers, being usually hindered by their reason and imagination, which create a thousand indecisions in deliberation and a thousand hesitations in execution. Those least apt or least accustomed to ponder or reflect are the most prompt to decide and in action the most efficient. But your own peers, who are always self-involved and powerless over themselves because overwhelmed, as it were, by the very amplitude of their own faculties, are almost always the slaves of irresolution both in thought and action, which is one of the great afflictions distressing human life. Add that by the excellence of your talents in hardly any time at all you will easily surpass almost all others of your species in branches of the most profound knowledge and in even the most difficult disciplines, yet you will always find it either impossible or extremely troublesome to learn or to put into practice many a thing trivial in itself but absolutely required in your relations with other men. At the same time you will see those very things performed perfectly and learned effortlessly by a thousand minds not only inferior to yours but altogether negligible. These and infinite other troubles and distresses occupy and besiege great minds. But these outstanding beings are rewarded abundantly by the fame, the praise, and the honors which their greatness earns them, and by the enduring remembrance they leave of themselves to posterity.

Soul: But those praises and honors you mention, will I get them from heaven, from you, or from whom?

Nature: From men, because none but they can give them.

Soul: Well imagine! And I thought that far from being praised I would be scorned and shunned by them as not knowing how to do the things most necessary, as you say, in human intercourse, and which even people with the poorest minds find easy, or that certainly I would live ignored by almost all of them, as unfit for human society.

Nature: It is not given me to foresee the future nor therefore to foretell infallibly what men will do and think about you while you are on earth. It is true though that, from my experience of the past, I deduce as on the whole likely that they will persecute you with envy, another of the calamities usually facing superior souls, or weigh you down with despite and indifference. Moreover, even fortune and chance itself are usually inimical to your kind. But immediately after you are dead, as occurred to one called Camoëns,[1] or at most a few years later, as happened to another called Milton, you will be exalted and extolled to heaven, I will not say by all but at any rate by the small number of men of judgment. And perhaps the ashes of the body in which you will have dwelt will rest in a magnificent sepulcher, and its likeness, variously reproduced, will be passed on from hand to hand. And many will recount and others with great industry will learn by heart the events of his life, and in the end all the civilized world will be filled with his name. If, that is, the malignity of fortune or the very superabundance of your faculties will not continually have hindered you from showing men some token proportional to your worth. Of this there has truly been no lack of examples known only to me and to fate.

[1] Naz de Camões, Portuguese poet. (Camoëns is the English spelling).

Soul: My dear mother, despite my present lack of further knowledge, nevertheless I feel that the greatest, or rather the only desire you have given me is the desire for happiness. But granting that I am capable of desiring glory, surely I cannot long for this—I don't know whether to say good or evil—except as there is happiness or value in acquiring it. Now though according to your own words it may well be a necessity or advantage in achieving glory, nevertheless the excellence with which you have endowed me does not lead to the achievement of happiness, rather it draws forcibly towards unhappiness. Nor does it seem plausible that before death it should lead me even to that very glory of which you speak, and after, what use or pleasure could come to me from the greatest good in the world? And in the end, as you yourself say, it may easily happen that the price of so much unhappiness, this so reluctant glory, may not be obtained for me anyway, even after death. So that I must conclude from your very own words that instead of singularly loving me, as you asserted in the beginning, you feel an anger and ill-will greater than men and fortune will feel towards me while I am in the world, since you have not hesitated to give me so calamitous a gift as this excellence you boast of. A gift that will be one of the main obstacles hindering me from attaining my sole end, which is happiness.

Nature: My dear daughter, as I have told you, all men's souls are the allotted prey of unhappiness, through no fault of mine. But in the universal misery of the human condition and in the infinite vanity of its every pleasure and advantage, the better part of mankind hold glory as the greatest good granted to mortals and the most worthwhile goal they can set for themselves to care about and to achieve. So that it is not out of hatred for you but out of genuine and singular goodwill that I have decided to give you all the assistance in my power to accomplish this end.

Soul: Tell me, among the lower animals you mentioned, does any one of them happen to be endowed with less vital power and sensitivity than man?

Nature: Beginning with those that retain in themselves something plantlike, though some are more so, some less, all are in this respect inferior to man, who has more abundant vitality and greater sensitivity than any other animal and is of all living creatures the most perfect.

Soul: Then if you love me, put me into the most imperfect. Of if you cannot, strip me of those disastrous gifts that ennoble me and make me into the most stupid and senseless human being you have ever produced.

Nature: Your last request I can satisfy and will, since you refuse imortality, for which I intended you.

Soul: And in exchange for that immortality I beg you to hasten my death as much as possible.

Nature: I shall have to confer with destiny about that.

GINO L. RIZZO & MILTON MILLER

DIALOGUE BETWEEN THE EARTH AND THE MOON

[DIALOGO DELLA TERRA E DELLA LUNA]

Earth: My dear Moon, I know that you can speak and answer me, since—as I've heard the poets say so often—you are a person. What's more, the children down here claim that you do, in fact, have a mouth, nose, and eyes; and that they can see this with their own eyes which, at their age, must be very sharp indeed. As for myself, I'm sure you realize that I am every bit as much a person as you. After all, in my younger days I did give birth to quite a few children. This being the case, you will hardly be surprised to hear me speak. At any rate, Moon dear, though I've been a neighbor of yours for more years than I can remember, I've never spoken to you till now because things have really kept me so busy that there was simply never time to chat. But nowadays my affairs take very little time—they practically take care of themselves—and I really don't know what to do with myself. In fact, I'm going out of my mind with boredom. That's why I hope to be speaking with you a good deal from now on, and taking an interest in your affairs; unless, of course, you have any objections.

Moon: Don't worry about that. I wish I could be as certain that Fate would keep me free from every displeasure as I am that you will cause me none at all. If you feel like chatting, go right ahead to your heart's content. Although, as I suppose you know, I am rather fond of silence, I'll give you an ear and be only too pleased to answer you if it will make you happy.

Earth: Tell me, then, do you hear that very pleasant music that the heavenly bodies make as they revolve through space?

Moon: No. Frankly I don't hear anything at all.

Earth: Neither do I, except for the noise of the wind blowing from my poles to the equator and back again; and that doesn't seem very musical to me. Still, Pythagoras says that the celestial spheres make such a lovely sound that it's a delight to hear them, and that even you have a part in it since you are the eighth string in what he calls the "universal lyre." But he also says that if I can't hear the sound it's simply because I'm deafened by it.

Moon: In that case I must be deafened by it too. As I told you, I don't hear any sound at all. And furthermore, I don't know anything about being a string in anyone's lyre.

Earth: Well then, let's change the subject. Tell me, are you really inhabited? Thousands of philosophers, ancient and modern ones from Orpheus to De la Lande, swear that you are. But no matter how far I stretch out these horns of mine—men call them mountains and peaks—and look at you through the tips, like a snail, I never manage to see a single living being.

They tell me, though, that a certain David Fabricius, whose sight was even sharper than Lynceus the Greek's, once discovered several of them spreading out their wash in the sun.

Moon: I can't say much about your horns. The fact is, however, I am inhabited.

Earth: What color are these men of yours?

Moon: What men?

Earth: Why, the ones who live on you. Didn't you say you were inhabited?

Moon: That's right. So?

Earth: Well, I assume that not all your inhabitants are animals, after all.

Moon: They're not animals, or men either. For that matter, I'm not even sure what kind of beings men and animals are. In fact, I haven't been able to make heads or tails out of all your talk about "men."

Earth: But what kind of people are they then?

Moon: All kinds, and there are many of them. You know as little about mine as I know about yours.

Earth: I must say that's all very strange. If I hadn't heard it from your own lips I never would have believed it. Another question: have you ever been conquered by any of these inhabitants of yours?

Moon: Not that I know of. What do you mean, "conquered?" How? Why?

Earth: I mean taken over through political trickery or by force of arms. You know, for selfish and ambitious reasons.

Moon: I don't know what any of this means: "political trickery," "force of arms," "ambitious reasons." Not a word of it.

Earth: Of course you do. At least, if you don't know what I mean by arms, you must know something about war. Why, not long ago one of our scientists down here took a look at you through his telescopes—that's what they call their devices that let them see things far away—and he saw that you had a fine fortress up there, with perfectly constructed bastions. Of course, this means that your people must be skilled in the attacks and defenses of siege warfare, if nothing else.

Moon: You will excuse me, Madam Earth, if my answer is perhaps a little less respectful than it should be, coming from one who is, after all, your subject—you might even say your servant. But the fact is, you do strike me as being a trifle conceited if you think that every other corner of creation must be just like your own; if you think that Nature had nothing better to do than use you as a model for everything else. First I tell you that I am inhabited, and immediately you jump to the conclusion that my inhabitants are men. Then I tell you that they are not, and although you accept the fact that they may be creatures of a different sort, you still persist in attributing to them the qualities of your own people, and assume that they live in a similar way. Then you talk to me about the telescopes of some scientist or other. But if these telescopes of yours give no clearer view of other things than they do of me, I'm afraid their vision is no better than that of the children down there who claim to see my eyes, mouth, and nose even though I'm sure I don't know where such things could possibly be.

Earth: Next you'll probably tell me there's no truth to the report that your provinces are clearly paved with broad avenues, or even that you've been cultivated, though it's perfectly easy to see both these things from Germany, through a telescope.

Moon: If I've been "cultivated," as you put it, I certainly don't know anything about it. And as for these avenues of mine, I for one have never seen them.

Earth: My dear Moon, I want you to know that, even though I haven't had much education, and may not be very bright—it's no wonder people are always playing tricks on me—even so, I can tell you a thing or two. For example, just because your own inhabitants haven't tried to conquer you, don't go thinking you've never been in danger. Why, there have been many times when people down here have thought about taking you over themselves. And they've made preparations to do it, too, more than once. If they haven't been successful yet it's only because they've never quite managed to reach you, even though they've stood on tiptoe on some of my highest points and stretched their arms way out. What's more, for some time now I've been watching people down here taking careful measurements of every part of you, drawing maps of your countries, figuring up the height of your mountains. In fact, down here they even know them all by name. I thought that, considering my affection for you, it was only right to let you know these facts just so you would never be caught unawares. Anyway, let's get down to other matters. Tell me, how do you put up with all the dogs that never stop howling at you? What do you think of people who delight in telling incredible lies, such as those who try to convince their friends that it is really you and not your reflection they see in the well? Are you male or female? In the olden days, you know, people were never quite sure. Is it true that the ancient Arcadians really came into the world before you, as they claimed? Is it true that your women —or whatever I should call them—produce their young from eggs, and that once upon a time one of these eggs fell down here on me? Do you really have a hole through your middle like a rosary-bead, as one of our scientists has been saying? Are you really made of green cheese? Certain Englishmen try to make us believe that you are. Is it true that one day—or was it one night?—Mahomet split you in two like a melon, and that a large chunk of you slid up his sleeve? Why do you take such pleasure in keeping close to the tops of minarets? And how do you feel about the Feast of Bairam?

Moon: Please don't stop now. While you go on like this I have no chance to answer you, and so I needn't break the silence I enjoy so much. If you like to talk nonsense and can't find anything else to say, you shouldn't waste your time with someone like me who doesn't understand you. Instead, you would do better to have these men of yours make another revolving moon for you, constructed and peopled to suit your taste. All you can speak about is men, and dogs, and other things of the sort. None of this means anything to me, any more than all the talk I hear about that tremendous sun they say our own sun revolves around.

Earth: It seems, in his discussion of ours, that the more I try to avoid speaking about myself and my own interests, the less I'm able to do so. I'll try to be more careful from now on. Now then, tell me, are you the one who has such a fine time making the water in my oceans rise and fall?

Moon: Perhaps. However, if I am the one who does this to you—or anything else, for that matter—it's certainly not conscious on my part. And I might say the same for you. You may not realize it, but you affect me in many ways too, and to a much greater degree, seeing how much larger you are than I.

Earth: I really don't know in what ways I could possibly affect you, except that once in a while I do deprive you of the sun's light, and at the same time deprive myself of yours. Also, I know that during your own nights I do shine quite brightly on you, for I have been able to notice this on many occasions. But I was almost forgetting the one queston that interests me more than all the rest. I'd like to know if Ariosto is right when he says that all the qualities that man keeps losing—his youth, his beauty, his health, the great pains he takes in search of fame, his efforts at bringing up his children properly and creating, or at least encouraging, useful occupations—if all these things leave mankind only to accumulate up there with you. If so, you must be a storehouse of all the human properties. (Except folly, of course; that's one that mankind never gives up.) If all this is true, it strikes me that you must be just about full, without much room to spare. For mankind has been losing a good many qualities, especially these days—patriotism, virtue, generosity, honesty. What's more, these qualities have not disappeared merely partially, and from a few—as was once the case—but completely and from everyone. Unless they've taken refuge up there with you, they are certainly not to be found anywhere at all. At any rate, I'd like to strike a bargain with you. Why don't you return all these things to me? Some you can give back right now, others little by little. I imagine you would be only too happy to get them off your hands, especially common sense, which must be taking quite a lot of room up there. In return I'll see to it that my people down here pay you a handsome amount each year.

Moon: People again! That's all you can talk about! Perhaps, as you say, folly never leaves your domain. But if you keep looking for all the common sense that your inhabitants have lost, you will, I'm afraid, make me lose my own. Believe me, I have no idea where their common sense can be, whether it has disappeared or still exists somewhere in creation. I only know that it is most definitely not up here. And neither are any of the other things you've been asking about.

Earth: Well, at least tell me this. Do you know anything up there above vice, crime, misfortune, pain, old age—in short, evil of every kind? Do these words mean anything to you?

Moon: They do indeed! I certainly do know the words you mention. What's more, I know only too well what they represent. I'm full to overflowing with just such things as these, rather than with all those other ones you had in mind.

Earth: Tell me then, which do you find more often among your inhabitants, moral strength or weakness?

Moon: Oh, weakness, by far!

Earth: And which is more common, good or evil?

Moon: Evil, unquestionably.

Earth: And your inhabitants? Are they happy or unhappy, in general?

Moon: Unhappy. In fact, they are so unhappy that I

wouldn't change places with the most contented one among them.

Earth: Likewise down here. In fact, what surprises me is that while you and I are so different in other ways, in this we're quite the same.

Moon: Let me take issue with you. I'm like you in many other ways too. Our forms are similar, we both revolve in the same way and receive our light from the sun. The resemblance you speak of is no more curious than these others. After all, evil is a quality shared by all the planets of the universe—or, at any rate, all those that revolve with us around our sun. It's no less common to us all than our round shape and the other conditions I've mentioned. If you could shout loudly enough to be heard by Uranus or Saturn, or any other planet of ours, and if you could ask whether they knew about unhappiness, and whether good or evil was more common among them, they would all answer as I have. I can say this with assurance because I've taken the opportunity of asking Venus and Mercury some of the same questions, being a little closer to them on occasion than you are. And, for that matter, I've even asked some of the comets that have passed by from time to time. All of them have given the same reply. In fact, I think the sun himself and even the stars would not answer any differently.

Earth: This may well be. Nevertheless, I'm optimistic, especially nowadays when these men of mine keep promising me that the future will be an age of great happiness.

Moon: Be optimistic if you like, from now till doomsday. I assure you nothing will come of it.

Earth: Wait! What's that? I think my men and animals are beginning to move about. As you can see—or should I say, as you cannot see—it's nighttime down here and they were all asleep. This discussion of ours must have awakened them. They're probably terrified by the noise.

Moon: But up here, as you can see, it's daytime.

Earth: At any rate, I certainly don't want to frighten these people of mine and rob them of their sleep. After all, it's the only comfort they have. We'll continue this some other time. Goodbye now, and a good day to you.

Moon: Goodbye. And good night.

NORMAN R. SHAPIRO

DIALOGUE BETWEEN NATURE AND AN ICELANDER

[DIALOGO DELLA NATURA E DI UN ISLANDESE]

An Icelander who had traveled over the greater part of the world, and lived in many countries, was once wandering in the heart of Africa, and crossed the equator in a place no man had ever seen before. There he had an adventure like the one that befell Vasco da Gama, who, as he rounded the Cape of Good Hope, watched that very Cape, guardian of the austral seas, loom up before him in the form of a giant in order to dissuade him from breaking those oceans through, where none before had sailed. In the distance he saw an enormous bust, which he at first thought was of stone, like the colossal figures seen by him many years before on Easter Island. But on closer inspection, he found it was the body of a woman of huge proportions, seated on the ground and holding herself erect by resting her back and elbows against a mountain. This was no statue, but a living person, with a face that inspired both admiration and terror, and jet black eyes and hair. She stared at him intently for some time, without speaking, but at last said:

Nature: Who are you? And what are you doing here, where no man has been before?

Icelander: I am a poor Icelander, fleeing from Nature, and having fled from her all my life to every corner of the globe, now I seek to escape her here.

Nature: So flies the squirrel from the rattlesnake, only to drop exhausted into the latter's jaws. I am she from whom you fly.

Icelander: Nature?

Nature: None other.

Icelander: That grieves me to the quick, for I am sure that nothing worse than this could happen.

Nature: It should have occurred to you that I might very well be here, where as you know, my power is greater than elsewhere. But what was it that made you flee?

Icelander: I must confess that after only a few experiences in early youth I became convinced of life's vanity and folly. I saw men engaged in a constant struggle to buy pleasures that bring no delight and goods that bring no joy; enduring and giving rise to countless pains and evils, which are troublesome and harmful at best; for in short, the farther they strayed from happiness, the more they sought to attain it. For these reasons, renouncing all other desires, I resolved to live an obscure and tranquil life, doing harm to no one, not striving to advance my fortune or contend with others in any way. Despairing of happiness as of something denied our species, I determined to avoid suffering at all costs. Not that I thought of abstaining from physical work or toil; for you are well aware of the difference between fatigue and discomfort, and between a quiet and an idle life. But as soon as I started to act on this resolution, I learned by experience how vain it is to think that by giving offense to no one, one may avoid being hurt by others, even by yielding spontaneously to all their demands and contenting oneself with what is least desirable in all things, including one's station in life, which, no matter how humble, must always be defended. But I easily freed myself from the cares of men by removing from their society, which in my native island may be done without difficulty. Living in solitude and

almost without a trace of joy, I could not escape suffering, be-
cause I was tormented by the long, cold winters and the short,
hot summers characteristic of the region, while the fire, next
to which I was compelled to spend most of my time, dried up
my flesh and filled my eyes with smoke; so, both indoors and
out, I could never save myself from perpetual discomfort, or
live the peaceful kind of life to which I had always aspired;
for the fearful storms on land and sea, the rumblings and
threatenings of Mount Hecla, and the dread of fires, which in
wooden dwellings like ours are constantly occurring, never
ceased to perturb me. Such trials as these, which are borne
with comparative ease when the mind is occupied with the
duties of social and civil life, or distracted by the bustle of
passing events, assume a much graver and more serious aspect
in a life of solitude, in which nothing is sought for but peace
and quiet. Seeing thus that the more I restricted, or rather con-
tracted, myself within myself in order not to harm or offend
anything in the world, the more troubled and disturbed I felt,
I resolved to change country and climate, in order to see if
there was anywhere on earth where, offending none, I might
live without being offended, and where, if I could not be
happy, I might at least not suffer. Another reason I was moved
to do this was because I thought that perhaps you had planned
for the human race (as you have done with many species of
animals and plants) to live in only one climate or region of the
globe; so that if men, contrary to your design, persisted in go-
ing beyond the bounds you assigned them, they might blame
their troubles not on you, but on themselves. Therefore I have
searched everywhere, and explored nearly every country, al-
ways keeping my resolution to do no harm to other creatures,
or the least possible, and to seek nothing for myself but a
peaceful life. But I have been burned with heat in the tropics,
curdled wth cold at the poles, suffered in the temperate zones
from the changeability of the weather, and been troubled
everywhere by elemental commotions. Then, too, I have seen

places where never a day goes by without a storm, which means that every day you attack the people who live there, who have never done you any harm. In other places there are calm skies above and earthquakes below, a furious multitude of volcanoes, and constant underground rumblings that shake the whole country. Winds and whirlwinds devastate the land. Sometimes I have felt the roof cave in over my head, laden with heavy snow; sometimes the rain fell so hard that the earth gave way under my feet; and often I have had to run for my life as fast as my feet would carry me from the floods that pursued me as if I had done them wrong. Wild beasts I had never harmed attempted to devour me; snakes tried to poison me; and in some places I only narrowly escaped being gnawed to the bone by flying insects. Not to speak of the countless everyday perils which are always threatening, for, as Seneca says, there's no cure for fear except the thought that everything is to be feared. Nor have I been spared any illness, though I have always been, and still am, not only temperate, but self-denying in all the pleasures of the flesh. I am struck with wonder when I consider that you have instilled in us such a firm and insatiable greed for pleasure that without it our lives are abortive and imperfect, while ordaining at the same time that the indulgence of this desire shall be, of all things human, the most hurtful to the health and strength of the body, the most calamitous in its general effects, and the most contrary to the duration of life itself. Nonetheless, though abstaining from almost every pleasure, I could not avoid suffering various and sundry ills, some of which threatened loss of life and limb, or even worse, all oppressing mind and body for days or months at a time with countless aches and pains. And though all men in time of sickness experience new and unaccustomed pains, and other torments besides (as if human life were not wretched enough at best), you have never given man, in compensation for this, any periods of exceptional or extraordinary good health from which he might derive some unalloyed pleasure. In countries where the ground is always blanketed with snow, I have been nearly blinded, a thing of frequent occurrence among the Laplanders. Sun and air, so vital and necessary to life, and therefore inescapable, harass us continually—one with its heat and even its light, the other with its humidity or its rigors; so that a man can never be exposed to either without more or less discomfort or harm. Indeed, I cannot remember spending a single day of my life free of suffering, while those I spent without even a trace of happiness are countless. Therefore I must conclude that you are the manifest enemy of mankind, of the other animals, and of all your works, since I realize that suffering is as much our destined and inevitable fate as unhappiness, and that it is as impossible to live a peaceful life of any kind as it is to lead an active one without misery; for now you ensnare us, now you threaten us, now you sting us, spite us, or rend us, and always you either injure or persecute us. Habit or fate has made you the slaughterer of your own family and children, and, in a manner of speaking, of your own flesh and blood. Thus I have abandoned all hope; for though men stop persecuting those who really want to hide or flee, you keep up your senseless pursuit until we are destroyed. Already I am approaching the bitter and sorrowful period of old age, a true and manifest evil, or rather, an accumulation of the worst evils and miseries; evils, moreover, not accidental, but decreed by you in laws for every living thing, foreseen by all of us even from childhood, and increasingly apparent from our twenty-fifth birthday on, so that, of human life, scarcely a third belongs to youth, only a few instants to maturity and perfection, and all the rest to old age and imminent decline.

Nature: Surely you don't think the world was made for you alone? You should realize that in my works, my laws, and my processes, with rare exceptions, I have never been especially concerned for man's happiness or unhappiness. When I cause you harm, I hardly ever mean to; for, ordinarily, if I please or help you, I don't know it; and despite what you may think, I have never altered my actions or behavior in order to please or help you. And, finally, if I happened to wipe out your species, I probably would not even notice.

Icelander: Suppose someone urged me to visit his home, and I went there to please him. Imagine, further, that on my arrival he lodged me in a rent and ruined cell, damp, fetid, and open to wind and rain, where I was constantly in danger of being crushed. Instead of taking the trouble to entertain me, or promoting my comfort, he provided just enough to keep me alive, and let me be insulted, mocked, threatened, and beaten by his children and family. Yet if I complained to him of such treatment, he might answer: "Did I build this house for you? Or do I keep my children and retainers just to serve you? I have other things to think about besides your comfort, or giving you good cheer." To this I might reply: You didn't build this house for me, yet it was in your power not to invite me. But since you asked me to come and stay here, don't you think it is up to you to make sure I am protected from danger and suffering? That's what I am saying now. I am well aware that you never made the world for the service of men. I rather think you made and ordered it for their torment. Now I ask you: Did I ever beg you to place me in this world? Did I intrude into it violently, against your will? But if you put me here without my knowledge or consent, isn't it your duty, if not to keep me happy and content, at least not to taunt and torture me, and let me live in peace? And I say this not only for myself, but for the whole human race, and every living thing.

Nature: Apparently it hasn't occurred to you that life in this universe is a perpetual cycle of production and destruction, so bound together that one is always counteracting the other, thus preserving the world, which, if either ceased to operate, would likewise dissolve. Therefore if man did not suffer, the world itself might be destroyed.

Icelander: That's the very argument I hear from all philosophers. But since what is destroyed suffers, and what destroys cannot be happy, but is soon destroyed in turn, tell me what no philosopher can tell me: For whose pleasure or profit does this most miserable life of the universe, preserved only at the cost of the death and suffering of all its component parts, exist?

While they were in the midst of debating these and similar problems, the story goes that two lions came upon the scene, so worn out and starved that they hardly had the strength to devour the Icelander, which they nonetheless did, and with that bit of nourishment, managed to live through the day. Some deny this, and say that as the Icelander spoke, a great, fierce wind arose, slapping him to the ground and burying him under a majestic pile of sand that dried him up perfectly, turning him into a fine mummy, which was later discovered by a group of travelers and placed in the museum of some town or other in Europe.

WILLIAM M. DAVIS

DIALOGUE BETWEEN FREDERICK RUYSCH AND HIS MUMMIES[1]

[DIALOGO DI FEDERICO RUYSCH E DELLE SUE MUMMIE]

Chorus of Corpses in the Cabinet of Frederick Ruysch:

> Alone eternal in the world, to which
> Created things all roll,
> In you, O death, there rests
> Our nature stripped of all;
> Not happy now, but safe
> From ancient suffering. The depth of night

Obscures the heavy thought
In the confused mind;
The arid spirit feels its breath depart
For hope and for desire:
Thus it is freed from fear and from distress,
And without tedium spends
The slow and empty years.
Before, we lived: and like some fearful ghost,
Confused remembrance of
Some weary dream that wanders in the mind
Of a mere suckling child:
Such is the memory we have
Of our own life; but fear is far away
When we recall. We were?
What was that bitter point
That had the name of life?
A wondrous mystery
Today is life within our thoughts, and such
As to the living seems
The thought of unknown death. And as in life
We fled away from death, so now far from
The vital flame of life
Our naked nature flees;
Not happy now, but safe;
For happiness by fate
Is still denied in dead and living state.

Ruysch (outside the laboratory, looking through the chink of the door): The deuce! Who has taught music to these corpses, singing like cocks at midnight? In truth I am in a cold sweat, and almost more dead than they are. I did not think they would revive, when I preserved them from corruption. Well so it is: with all my philosophy, I am trembling from head to foot. Curse that devil who tempted me to bring these into my house. What can I do? If I leave them here shut up, may they not break down the door, or come out by the keyhole to seek me out in bed? To call for help for fear of corpses does not become me. Come, a little courage, let's try to frighten them a bit.

(Going in.) My lads, what is the game? Have you forgotten that you're dead? What is this hubbub? Have you grown proud because of the visit from the Czar,[2] and think that you're not subject to the laws as you were? I imagine that you meant to jest, and weren't in earnest. If you are resuscitated, I'm delighted; but I'm not so rich that I can keep the living, as the dead; and so, be off with you. If what they say of vampires is true, and you are of that sort, then look for other blood to drink: for I'm not disposed to let my own be sucked as liberally as if it were the artificial blood that I have put into your veins.[3] In short, if you continue to be peaceful and silent, as you have been till now, we shall keep on good terms, and you shall lack for nothing in my house; if not, take warning that I shall pick up this iron bar from off the door, and kill you all.

A Corpse: Don't be angry; for I promise you that we will all stay dead, without your killing us.

Ruysch: Then what is this idea that came to you just now, to sing?

Corpse: Just now, on the stroke of midnight, was completed for the first time that great mathematical year of which the ancients write so much; and this likewise is the first time that the dead speak. And not only us, but in every cemetery in every tomb, down in the bottom of the sea, under the snow or sand, under the open sky, and in whatever place they are, all the dead, at midnight, sang as we did that little song you heard.

Ruysch: And how long will they go on singing or talking?

Corpse: They have already finished snging. They have the power to talk for a quarter of an hour. Then they return to silence till the same year is once again complete.

Ruysch: If this is true, I don't think you will break my sleep again. Speak freely then among yourselves; for I will stand aside, and gladly listen to you, out of curiosity, without disturbing you.

Corpse: We cannot talk otherwise than by way of answer to someone who is alive. Those who have no answer to make to the living, when the song is ended, remain quiet.

Ruysch: I'm very sorry: for I think it would be most pleasant to hear what you said amongst yourselves, if you could speak together.

Corpse: Even if we could, you would hear nothing; for we should have nothing to say to each other.

Ruysch: A thousand questions to put to you come into my mind. But since the time is short, and leaves no room for choice, explain to me in brief what feelings you had in body and in mind at the point of death.

Corpse: I never was aware of the actual point of death.

The Other Corpses: Nor were we.

Ruysch: How could you not notice it?

Corpse: For example, as you never notice the moment that you fall asleep, however much attention you may give to it.

Ruysch: But falling asleep is a natural thing.

Corpse: And does not dying seem natural to you? Show me a man, an animal, a plant, that does not die.

Ruysch: I am no longer surprised that you go on singing and talking, if you did not notice you were dead.

> *So he, not noticing the blow*
> *Continued fighting, although dead,*

as an Italian poet says. I thought that you knew something more about death than do the living. But then, to come back to the matter, you felt no pain in the instance of death?

Corpse: What pain can that be which he who feels it does not notice?

Ruysch: At any rate, all are convinced that the feeling of death is very painful.

Corpse: As if death was a feeling, and not the opposite.

Ruysch: And both those who hold with the Epicureans about the nature of the soul, and those who hold the normal view, all, or the majority, agree in what I say; that is, in thinking death to be by its own nature, and without comparison, the sharpest pain.

Corpse: Well, you may ask of us: If man has not the power to realise the point in which the vital operations, to a greater or less extent, remain no more than interrupted, either by sleep or lethargy or syncope or any other cause, how can he notice that in which those same operations cease altogether, and not for a short while, but for ever? Apart from that, how can a living feeling find place in death? Or rather, death itself be by its own quality a living feeling? When the power of feeling is not only weakened and scanty, but reduced to such a minimum that it fails and is annulled, do you imagine the person capable of a strong feeling? Or rather, this very extinguishing of the power to feel, do you think that it can be a very great feeling? Yet you see that even those who die of acute and painful ills, at the approach of death, more or less time before they expire, grow calm and rest in such a way that one can know their life, reduced to a small quantity, is not sufficient for pain, so that this ceases sooner than that. This you may say from us to anyone who fears to die of pain at the point of death.

Ruysch: For the Epicureans perhaps these reasons will be enough. But not for those who judge otherwise of the substance of the soul, as I have done in the past, and shall do all the more now that I've heard the dead talking and singing. Because, considering that dying consists in separation of the soul from the body, they will not understand how these two things, conjoined and as it were conglutinated together so as to form one and the other a single person, can be separated without very great violence, and unspeakable travail.

Corpse: Tell me: Is the spirit stuck perhaps in the body by some nerve, some muscle or membrane, that has necessarily to break when the spirit goes? Do you not see that the soul only leaves the body because it is prevented from staying there, and has no place there any more; not through any force that tears and roots it out? Tell me further: perhaps on entry, it feels itself stuck or stoutly tied, or as you say conglutinated? Why then should it feel itself unstuck when it departs, or let us say, experience a very vehement sensation? Rest assured, the entry and the exit of the soul are equally quiet, easy, soft.

Ruysch: Then what is death, if it's not pain?

Corpse: Rather a pleasure than ought else. Know that to die is as to fall asleep, it does not happen in a single instant, but by degrees. It is true that these degrees are more or less, and greater or smaller, according to the varied causes and the sorts of death. In the final of these instants death does not bring either any pain or any pleasure, any more than sleep. In the other ones before, it cannot generate pain: for pain is a living thing, and the senses in that time, that is, when death has commenced, are moribund, which is to say, extremely attenuated in their strength. It may well be the cause of pleasure: for pleasure is not always a living thing; rather perhaps the greater part of man's delights consist in some sort of languidness. So that the senses are capable of pleasure even when near to extinction; since very often languor is itself a pleasure; especially when it frees from suffering; since you well know that the cessation of any pain or discomfort is a pleasure in itself. So that the languor of death must be more welcome according as it frees a man from greater suffering. For my part, though in the hour of death I did not give much attention to what I felt, because my doctors forbade me to tire my brain; yet I remember that the sensation which I felt was not much unlike the pleasure caused to men by the languor of sleep, in that moment when they are drowsing off.

The Other Corpses: We also seem to remember that.

Ruysch: It may be as you say: although all those with whom I have had occasion to talk about this matter thought very differently: But, so far as I can recollect, they did not allege their own experiences. Now tell me: In the time of death, while you felt this sweetness, did you think that you were dying, and that this pleasure was a courtesy of death; or did you imagine some other thing?

Corpse: So long as I was not dead, I was never persuaded that I should not manage to avoid that danger; and if no more, right to the last point when I had power to think, I hoped an hour or two of life would still be left: as I think happens with many when they die.

The Other Corpses: That is what happened to us.

Ruysch: And so Cicero says[4] that there is no one so decrepit that he does not promise himself to live at least a year. But how did you notice at the last that the sprit had left the body? Say: how did you know that you were dead?

(They do not answer.) My lads, do you not hear? The quarter-hour must have gone by. Let's feel them a little. They're dead again all right: there is no danger of them frightening me again a second time: so let's go back to bed.

J.H. WHITFIELD

NOTES

1. See, among others, concerning these famous mummies: Fontenelle, *Eloge de Monsieur Ruysch.*
2. Ruysch's cabinet was twice visited by Czar Peter I, who later, having bought it, transferred it to St. Petersburg.
3. Ruysch preserved his corpses by injection of a certain substance made up by him, which had wonderful effects.
4. *De Senectute,* cap. 7.

DIALOGUE BETWEEN CHRISTOPHER COLUMBUS AND PEDRO GUTIÉRREZ

[DIALOGO DI CRISTOFORO COLOMBO E DI PIETRO GUTIÉRREZ]

Columbus: What a beautiful night, my friend.

Gutiérrez: Indeed it is, although I must say it would be even more beautiful on land.

Columbus: So! You too have become tired of life at sea, have you?

Gutiérrez: No, no. It's not the life at sea I mind; not really. It's only that this particular voyage seems to be taking longer than I ever expected and it's beginning to wear on me. Even so, don't think I'm complaining, like the others, mind you. Not at all. Whatever you decide to do, I'll stand behind you to the last, as I always have. You can be sure of that. Still, as long as we are on the subject, I do wish you would tell me, sincerely, if you are as convinced now as you were before that there's land in this part of the world, or if all this time spent with no results has begun to give you some doubts.

Columbus: Let me speak frankly, as I think I may with so trusted a friend. If you must know, I am less confident than I used to be, and with good reason. In the first place, several indications that had raised my hopes earlier now have proved vain. For example, you recall the birds that came flying in from the west a few days out of Gomera, and which I took as a sign of land not far off. That was my first deception. Then too, I have noticed, day after day, that facts have failed to bear out several of the conjectures and predictions I had formulated before sailing, about our probable experiences at sea. And so, I have begun to reason with myself that, if I was mistaken in these predictions—which had seemed almost irrefutable—I might just as easily be mistaken in my principal conjecture, namely that there is land beyond the Ocean. And yet, this conjecture is based on such foundations that if it should be disproved, it seems to me that we could hardly trust our human judgment at all, except for what we can see and touch directly. But on the other hand, I realize that theory and fact are often at odds— indeed, more often than not. "What makes you think," I ask myself, "that there is any similarity at all between various parts of the world? Why must you assume that, simply because the eastern hemisphere is divided between land and sea, the western hemisphere must be also? How can you be sure that it is not occupied merely by one immense body of water, or indeed by some element other than land or water? Or, even if it does contain both, like the other hemisphere, may it not be uninhabited, or even uninhabitable? And granting that it is no less inhabited than our own, how can you be sure that its inhabitants are equally rational? And if they are, what makes you think they are men rather than some other sort of thinking animal? Indeed, if they are men, might they not be completely different from the ones you know? For example, they might be of greater size, strength, and agility, favored by Nature with far more wit and good sense. Might they not be more civilized, and more advanced in both art and science?" These are the questions I have been asking myself. The power of Nature, after all, is so vast, and its effects so numerous and diverse, that we cannot judge with any certainty what it has accomplished—and may even now be accomplishing—in this unknown region far removed from our own. We may even wonder if it is not a mistake to predict conditions in one on the basis of the other. It is not at all unreasonable, I think, to imagine the unknown world full of things which—in part at least—would strike us as curious and bewildering. For example, here in these waters we have already observed with our own eyes a new phenomenon, unknown to seamen before us: our compass needle deflects from the north star a good deal toward the west. No matter what reasons I invent for this strange behavior, none satisfies me. And yet, I do not for a moment suggest that we should lend an ear to the

fables of the ancients about the wonders that abound in un-
known lands and in this very ocean; fables like those that
Hanno told of countries where flames filled the dark of night,
and where rivers of raging fire rushed headlong to the sea. We
have already seen how groundless were the fears that gripped
our men who thought they saw new and terrifying miracles all
about them. Recall, for example, that great mass of seaweed, so
thick that it seemed to transform the water into a meadow, and
kept us from moving ahead. Our men were certain that we had
reached the ultimate limits of the navigable sea. At any rate, to
answer your question, let me say merely this: although my con-
jecture is based on most probable assumptions, not merely in
my own judgment, but in that of the many distinguished geog-
raphers, astronomers, and navigators whom I consulted in
Spain, Italy, and Portugal—as you well know—still, it may
quite possibly be incorrect. As I have said before, the most sub-
stantial conclusions drawn from the best reasonings, fail to
withstand the test of experience, especially when these deal
with phenomena about which little is known.

Gutiérrez: What you are telling me, in effect, is that you have
risked your life, and the lives of your comrades, for nothing but
an opinion which may well be unfounded.

Columbus: True enough: I canot deny it. But, apart from the
fact that men risk their lives every day for far less weighty is-
sues, and indeed for matters of no concern at all—and even
without realizing the risk they are taking—consider the ques-
tion from another point of view. If, at this moment, you and I
and all our comrades were not on this ship, in the midst of this
sea, and this unknown solitude; if we were not threatened with
all the uncertainty and perils you care to name, what kind of
life would we be having? What would we be doing? How would
we be spending our days? More cheerfully, do you think? I
suspect, on the contrary, that we might find ourselves faced
with even greater trouble or hardship; or else, bored to death.
What do we mean by a life free from uncertainty and peril? If

really against boredom

we mean a truly happy and contented one, then such a life is, indeed, preferable to any other. But if we mean nothing but a tedious and miserable existence, I can imagine no life that would be less desirable. I care not to mention the glory that will be heaped upon us, and the service we shall do mankind, if our venture succeeds according to our hope. Yet, even if we accomplish nothing else by our voyage, it seems to me that it will have been of utmost value in that it has, for a time, freed us from the boredom of inaction, and made us appreciate the value of our lives and of many things we might otherwise have held in low esteeem. No doubt you have read, or heard, the tale the ancient writers tell. Unhappy lovers, they say, would leap into the sea from the rock of Santa Maura—known to Antiquity as the Leucadian rock. If they remained unharmed, they would, through Appollo's mercy, be forever free from the torments of love. Now then, I hardly know if we can believe that they were, in fact, thus rewarded. But I do know this: Once out of danger, they must have prized, at least for a little while, that very life they had scorned; or at any rate they must have prized it more dearly than before. And this, without Apollo's help, to be sure. To my mind every voyage is rather like a leap from the Leucadian rock. It produces the same fortunate effect, though a far more lasting one. For this reason it is to be preferred. It is a common notion that sailors and soldiers attach less importance to life than anyone else, since they are always so close to losing it. On the contrary, it is for this very reason, I think, that few people value life so much. What a wealth of blessings mankind lets pass unnoticed! Yet, for the man of the sea, these—and even the commonest things that others would scarcely call blessings—are dear beyond measure, only because he is deprived of them! How many men would be thankful for a bit of earth to stand upon? None but the seafaring men, and ourselves foremost among them. For, not knowing what the result of our voyage may be, our most fervent wish is merely to sight a patch of land. Such is our first thought when we wake and our last as we fall asleep. And if, one day, we catch the distant sight of a mountain peak, or the topmost branches of a forest, or anything of the sort, our joy will know no bounds. If, then, we should reach land, the very knowledge that we are again on solid ground and may go about as we please, will, for many a day, make us feel that we are indeed among the blessed.

Gutiérrez: What you say is undeniable. I must admit that if your theory proves as sound as the arguments you use to defend it, we shall all enjoy such blessedness one day.

Columbus: I for one shall keep hoping that we may enjoy it before long, though I no longer dare expect it. For several days now, as you know, the sounding-line has touched bottom, and has brought to the surface material whose appearance gives me some hope. Then too, the clouds that circle the sun toward evening seem different in shape and color from the ones we have seen before. The air—you may have noticed—is a little warmer and more gentle than it used to be. Even the wind is abating. It no longer blows steadily in one direction, as before, but seems instead to fluctuate as if some obstacle were in its path. There have been other hopeful signs as well: the stalk of cane that come floating by and that looked as if it had been only recently cut; and that little branch with its fresh red berries. Then too, I am encouraged by the flocks of birds that have been flying overhead. Although they aroused only false hopes before, they now appear day after day, and in such number that I think we may be able to put some faith in them; especially since I have noticed among them many which do not look like sea birds. Try as I may to restrain my enthusiasm, all these signs have given me great hope.

Gutiérrez: God grant this time that it may be fulfilled.

NORMAN R. SHAPIRO

THE SONG OF THE WILD COCK

[CANTICO DEL GALLO SILVESTRE]

There are Hebrew scholars and writers who affirm that between heaven and earth, or let us say, half in the one and half in the other, there lives a certain wild cock, whose feet are on the ground, while with its beak and crest it touches the sky. This giant cock, apart from various things that can be read about it in the aforesaid authors, has the use of reason; or indeed, like a parrot, it has been taught, by whom I know not, to utter words in the manner of men: for there has been found in an ancient parchment, written in Hebrew script, and in language a mixture of Chaldean, Aramaic, Rabbinical, Cabalistic, and Talmudic, a canticle entitled *Scir detarnegòl bara letzafra*, which is to say, *Morning Song of the Wild Cock*; and this, not without great labor, and recourse to more than one Hebrew rabbi, cabalist, theologian, jurist, and philosopher, I have contrived to understand, and to translate, as hereafter can be seen. I cannot yet discover if this song is repeated by the cock from time to time, or every morning; or whether it was sung once only; nor who hears it sung, or has heard it; nor if this language is really that of the cock, or whether the Song was translated into it from some other tongue. As for the translation which follows, to make it as faithful as was possible (and to do this I endeavored in every other way I could), I thought it best to use prose rather than verse, though the subject is poetic. The abrupt style, at times perhaps bombastic, must not be held against me, since it conforms to the original text and this text corresponds in this particular to the usage of the languages, and especially of the poets, of the orient.

Up, mortals, awake! The day is born again: truth returns to earth, and empty images depart. Arise; resume the burden of your life; come back from the false into the real world!

Each in this time collects, reviews within his mind, all the thoughts of his present life; recalls to his memory his plans, his studies, and his business; represents to himself the pleasures and distresses that will come to him in the space of the new day. And each in this time is more desirous than ever to find in his mind happy expectations and sweet thoughts. But few are satisfied in this desire: for all, to awaken is an evil. The wretch no sooner is awake than he returns into the hands of his unhappiness. Sleep is the sweetest thing, which brings with it a sense of joy and hope. One and the other are preserved whole and safe until the dawning of the following day; but in this they fail, or dwindle.

If the sleep of mortals were perpetual, and the same thing as life; if under the day star, while all the living languished in deepest quiet over the earth, no activtiy appeared; neither the lowing of oxen in the fields, nor the roar of wild beasts in the forests, nor the song of birds in the air, nor any murmur of bees or butterflies ran through the countryside; if no voice, nor any movement than that of waters, winds, and storms, arose on any side; the world would be pointless, of course; but would there be perhaps a lesser quantity of happiness, or more of misery, than now is found? O sun, author of the day, guardian of our waking hours, I ask of you: In all the centuries that you have marked and consummated, rising and setting to this day, did you once see one only amongst those living who was blest? Out of the innumerable acts of mortals which you have seen till now, do you think that there was even one achieved its end, the satisfaction, durable or transitory, of that creature who produced it? Or rather, do you see now, or did you ever see, happiness within the confines of the world? In what field does it dwell, in what wood, what mountain, what valley, what land inhabited or desert, in which planet of the myriads your flames light up and warm? Maybe it is hidden from your sight, resides in the depths of caverns, or at the bottom of the earth or sea?

What living thing partakes of it; what plant or other thing you vivify; what creature endowed or unprovided with vegetative or animal life? And you yourself, you who like a tireless giant, swiftly, day and night, with neither sleep nor rest, run the boundless race which is prescribed to you; are you blessed or unhappy?

Mortals, awake! You are not yet free from life. The time wll come when no outside force, no inward movement, will shake you from the quietness of sleep; but you will rest for ever insatiably in it. Death is not granted to you yet; Only from time to time and for a little while a semblance of it is given to you. For life could not be preserved were it not interrupted frequently. To lack too long this sort and failing sleep is in itself a mortal ill, the cause of everlasting sleep. Such is the nature of life, that to bear it one must now and again, by laying it down, redraw a little breath, refresh oneself with a taste and as it were a particle of death.

It seems that the existence of things has as its proper and its only object dying. Since that which never existed could not die, therefore all existing things have sprung out of nothingness. Certainly the final purpose of existence is not happiness; for no thing is happy. True it is that living creatures set themselves this end in all their works; but from none do they attain it; and in all their life, contriving, striving, toiling ever, in truth they only suffer, only labor, to arrive at this one intent of Nature, which is death.

At least, the first moment of the day is wont to be the most tolerable for the living. Few on awaking find in their minds happy and delightful thoughts; but almost all produce and form some now: for in this moment the mind, especially without a specific and particular preoccupation, is inclined above all to cheerfulness, or more disposed than at another time to patience towards ills. Therefore if anyone, when he was caught by sleep, had been filled with despair; when he awakes, he receives again hope in his mind, even if it in no wise fits his case. Many misfortunes and troubles of our own, many reasons for fear and for distress, seem at that time much smaller than they seemed the night before. Often also, the anguish of the day before is turned to scorn, almost to laughter, as the result of errors, empty imaginings. The evening is like old age; and as an opposite, the beginning of the morning is like youth: this for the most part consoled and confident; the evening sad, discouraged, given to forebodings. But as the youth of all our life, so that which mortals live on every day is very brief and fugitive; and soon the day too turns for them to elder age.

The flower of our years, though it is the best of life, is yet a poor thing. Nevertheless, even this little good fails in so short a time, that when the creature sees by many signs the decline of his own being scarcely has he experienced its perfection, or been able to feel and know completely his own powers, before they fail. With whatever kind of mortal creatures, the greatest part of living is a withering away. So much in all her works is Nature bent on, turned to, death: since for no other reason does old age prevail so clearly, and so much, in life and in the world. Each part of the universe hastens unwearyingly towards death, with marvelous solicitude and celerity. Only the universe itself appears immune from decay and languishing: for if in autumn and winter it shows itself almost infirm and old, yet always it grows young again with spring. But just as mortals, though in the first part of the day they re-acquire some part of youth, yet every day grow old, and finally expire; just so the universe, though in the beginning of the year it grows young, yet continually it ages. The time will come when this universe, and Nature herself, will be no more. And in the same way as of great kingdoms and empires of mankind, and their wondrous works, far-famed in other ages, there is now no sign nor any name; so of the whole world, and of the infinite vicissitudes and calamities of created things, no vestige will remain; but a bare silence, and a deepest stillness, will pervade the immensity of space. Thus this dread and wondrous mystery of universal life, before it has been declared or understood, will vanish and be lost.*

* This is a poetic, and not a philosophic, conclusion. Speaking philosophically, existence never having begun will never end. [Note by Leopardi]

J.H. WHITFIELD

COPERNICUS

[IL COPERNICO]

SCENE ONE

First Hour: Good morning, Your Excellency.

Sun: Yes, and good night too.

First Hour: Your horses are ready.

Sun: Good.

First Hour: The dawn's already out a little.

Sun: Good. Let it come or go if it wants to.

First Hour: What does Your Excellency mean?

Sun: I mean—I want you to let me alone.

First Hour: But—Your Excellency—the night's already lasted so long it can't go on much longer. And if we put it off, Your Excellency, something strange is going to happen.

Sun: Let whatever happens happen.

First Hour: O, Your Excellency, what does this mean? Aren't you feeling well?

Sun: No. No. I'm not feeling *anything*. I just don't want to budge. So go take care of your business.

First Hour: How can I take care of my business if you won't come too? I'm the first hour of the day. How can the day begin if Your Excellency won't step outside the way you always do?

Sun: If you can't be the first hour of the day, then you'll have to be the first hour of the night. Or else the night hours will have to work overtime. You and your day friends can have some time off. Do you want to know why? I'm tired of all this going around making light for a handful of beasts who live on a handful of mud that's so tiny I—with my perfect vision—can't even see it. Well, tonight I've stopped caring about it. If men want to see some light, let them keep their fires burning or find some other way.

First Hour: But, Your Excellency, how do you expect the poor things to survive? And if they have to keep their lamps burning or get candles to burn all day long, the cost will be exorbitant. If they'd discovered that gas to light up streets and rooms and shops and taverns and everything else—all at a reasonable price—then I'd say they weren't so badly off. But the fact is—it's going to take about three hundred years before they discover that cure. Meanwhile, they're going to run out of oil and wax and pitch and tallow, and they won't have anything left to burn.

Sun: They can go out and catch fireflies or other insects that light up.

First Hour: But how can they fight off the cold? Without help from Your Excellency, all the forests in the world won't be enough to keep them warm. And besides, they'll die of hunger, because the earth won't produce any more crops. And after a few years, the whole race of those poor animals will disappear. Once they've groped around a little here and there, looking for something to eat or something to keep them warm, finally when everything's eaten that could satisfy them, and the last spark of fire's consumed—finally they'll all pass away in the dark, frozen like so many bits of rock crystal.

Sun: What do I care? Am I the wet-nurse of the human race? Or the cook, who seasons their food? Why should I care if a certain group of invisible creatures, millions of miles away from me, can't see or can't ward off the cold without my light? And furthermore, if I have to serve as an oven or a fireplace for the human race, it's certainly reasonable for the family to group itself around the fireplace if it wants to keep warm—not for the fireplace to go whirling around the family. And so if the Earth needs my presence, let *it* come to me and do the asking. *I* certainly don't need to go to it and ask for anything.

First Hour: Your Excellency means—if I understand correctly—that the Earth should now do what you've done in the past.

Sun: Right. Now and forever after.

First Hour: I'm sure Your Excellency's right in this matter—especially since you can look after yourself. Nevertheless, Your Excellency, please try to consider how many wonderful things have to be discarded to usher in this new order of things. The day won't have its golden chariot any more with its beautiful horses bathing in the ocean. And—forgetting all the other details—we poor hours won't have a place in the heavens any more. We'll change from heaven's children to Earth's. In fact, I'm afraid we might just go up in smoke. But, be this as it may, the main difficulty will be to persuade the Earth to start moving around. And that ought to be pretty hard because the Earth's not used to it. It's going to seem strange for it to have to run and exert itself so much, considering it hasn't budged an inch from its seat up to now. And if Your Excellency's really lending an ear to laziness—as it now seems —I can tell you the Earth's not one bit more inclined to work these days than it was in the past.

Sun: In that case, necessity will goad it, and make it leap and run the way it ought to. But anyway, the surest, quickest solution is to find a poet—or maybe a philosopher—to persuade the Earth to move. And if that's not possible, then get it moving by force. Because in the last analysis, these matters all rest in the hands of poets and philosophers. They can do almost the whole job for us. Poets are the people who won my goodwill in the past—when I was young and listened to them. They got me—big and fat as I am—to take on this silly job of running around a measly grain of sand. Because I either felt it was a pleasure or a duty. But now I've grown up. I've turned toward philosophy myself. I look for the useful in things—not the beautiful. And the conceits of the poets just make me laugh —when they aren't turning my stomach. Whenever I act, I want to have some valid reasons—reasons with substance behind them. And I can't see any reason for preferring an active life to a life of pleasure and ease. There's no just reward for toil—and so I've decided to give up my straining and struggling for others. As far as I'm concerned, I'm going to live at home in peace and quiet. Aside from my age, which I've already mentioned, I've been influenced by philosophers—a breed that's fast gaining in importance, and is going to gain more and more every day. Since we want the Earth to move around and take my place, we might consider a poet instead of a philosopher to help us. After all, poets use one innocuous story after another to make people believe that things have value and importance, and are pleasant and extremely beautiful. By creating a thousand joyous hopes, they often make other people want to work. Philosophers never do that. But on the other hand, since philosophers are getting the upper hand, I doubt that the Earth would listen to a poet any more than I would. Or if it did listen, that it would produce any resuls. And so we'd better consult a philosopher. Even if philosophers usually aren't very active or willing to make other people act, in this extreme case they just might do something extraordinary. Unless the Earth would rather go to ruin than exert itself—and I can't really say I'd blame it—but, that's enough. Let's see what happens. This is your job. Go to the Earth—or let me send one of your friends. Whichever you like. And if she finds one of those philosophers standing outside his house studying the sky and stars—as she certainly ought to, considering how peculiar this extra-long night is—she should lift him up, toss him on her back, and bring him here to me. Then I'll explain to him what's going on in the world. Understand?

First Hour: Yes, Your Excellency. It will be done.

SCENE TWO

(Copernicus is standing on the terrace of his house, gazing at the eastern sky through a small paper tube. Telescopes haven't yet been invented.)

Copernicus: What a terrific thing! Either the clocks are all wrong or the sun ought to be up an hour already. I can't see a single streak in the east, even though the sky's as clear and polished as a mirror. The stars are twinkling as if it were midnight. Better check the Almagest and Sacrobosco. Find out the cause of this phenomenon. I've heard a lot about that long night Jupiter spent with the wife of Amphitryon. And I remember reading in that recent book by that Spaniard how the Peruvians tell of a long night in the past—an endless one— before the sun finally rose out of a lake they call Titicaca. But up to now I thought all this was nonsense. In fact, I was sure it was nonsense—just like any other rational man. To tell the truth, I can see now that reason and science aren't worth a damn. From now on I'm going to believe that these things and others like them are the essence of truth. In fact, I'm going to all the lakes and swamps to see if I can fish up the Sun. But what's that whirring—like the wings of a gigantic bird?

SCENE THREE

Last Hour: Copernicus, I'm the last hour.

Copernicus: The last hour? Well, I'll have to submit. Only, if I may, give me a little time to draw up my will and put my affairs in order before I die.

Last Hour: Die? What do you mean? I'm not the last hour of life.

Copernicus: Well, what are you then? The last hour of mass?

Last Hour: I'm sure that's your favorite hour—especially when you're up in the choir.

Copernicus: How did you know I was a clergyman? And how did you know my name?

Last Hour: I got my information about you from some people down below there, in the street. Well, I'll tell you. I'm the last hour of the day.

Copernicus: Ah! Now I understand. The first hour's sick. That's why the day hasn't begun yet.

Last Hour: Let me do the talking. The day's never going to start again—not today, not tomorrow, and never after—unless you see to it.

Copernicus: Now that's just fine. *Me*—making the day!

Last Hour: I'll tell you how. But first you've got to come with me to the Sun's house. He's my boss. You'll learn more of it on the way. His Excellency will explain the rest when we're there.

Copernicus: Sounds good. But if I'm not mistaken, the trip's going to be a long one. How can I take enough food so I won't starve to death before I get there? I understand Your Excellency's estates don't have enough food to give me a single lunch.

Last Hour: Don't worry about that. You won't be there long. And the trip will be over in a second. In case you don't know it, I'm a spirit.

Copernicus: Yes, but I'm a body.

Last Hour: Well, you shouldn't get all tangled up in talk like this because you're not a metaphysician yet. Come over here. Climb on my shoulders. Let me do the rest.

Copernicus: Well, here I go—let's see now the end of this adventure!

SCENE FOUR

Copernicus: Most Illustrious Lord.

Sun: Pardon me, Copernicus, if I don't ask you to sit. Here we don't have any chairs. But we'll cover everything quickly. You've already heard the whole business from my maid. As far as I'm concerned—and from what the girl told me about you—I think you're the perfect man for the job in question.

Copernicus: Your Lordship, I see a lot of trouble in this business.

Sun: Trouble shouldn't make a man like you afraid. They say trouble gives the high-spirited more spirit. But go on, what trouble were you thinking of?

Copernicus: First of all, though philosophy's power is strong, I'm not sure it's strong enough to persuade the Earth to start moving, instead of sitting there at ease. To start getting tired, instead of remaining in idleness. Especially in this age, which is by no means heroic.

Sun: Well, if you can't persuade it, force it.

Copernicus: Gladly, Your Lordship—if I were a Hercules or even a Roland. But I'm just a clergyman from Varmia.

Sun: What's that got to do with it? Can't you remember that ancient mathematician who was sure he could move heaven and earth if he could stand somewhere outside the earth? Well, you don't have to move heaven. But here. Look. You're outside the earth. And unless you're no match for that ancient, you shouldn't have any trouble moving the Earth—whether it likes it or not.

Copernicus: Your Lordship, I could do it, but I'd need a lever . . . a lever so long that not even you or I—no matter how rich you are, my lord—could afford even half the expense for its materials and labor cost. But now I'll tell you a worse problem. A knot of a problem. Up to now, the Earth's been sitting in the front row of the Universe—or we might say, the middle. And as you know, it's been standing motionless with nothing to do but look around at all the other globes in the Universe—big and small, dark and shiny—that go whirling around it, above it, below it, and on its sides continually, swiftly, assiduously, so furiously it's enough to overwhelm you just thinking about it. And since they all seemed ready to offer their services, the Earth considered the Universe its court. The Earth seemed to be sitting on a throne—with the other celestial spheres grouped around it like courtiers and guards and servants, performing one job after another. As a result, the Earth considered itself ruler of the world. And surely when things stood that way in the past, you could hardly blame it. Even I wouldn't deny that this conceit had a poor foundation. Well, what shall I say about men? We thought of ourselves—as we probably always will—as being more than the first and most important of earthly creatures. Every one of us—even if he wore a pair of patched pants and didn't have a crust to nibble on—considered himself an emperor. And not just the emperor of Constantinople or Germany or half of the world—like the Romans—but the emperor of the Universe . . . of the Sun, the planets and the stars, visible or not. And the final cause for the stars and the planets and your own illustrious realm and everything else. But now if we want to make the Earth move from the central place, if we want to make it run, revolve, toil like the other heavenly bodies—in other words, become one of the planets—then the Earthly Majesty and the Human Majesties will have to descend from their thrones and abandon their empire. They'll have to be content with their rags and miseries—and those miseries aren't few.

Sun: What conclusion are you drawing from this talk, my dear Sir Nicholas? Perhaps you have scruples? You think it's high treason?

Copernicus: No, Your Lordship. I can't remember that any of the codices or digests or books of public law or imperial law or civil law or natural law mention a high treason like this. But let me say that our job won't just be physical—the way it looks at first. The results won't just upset physics. No. They'll upset the whole great chain of the values of things and the hierarchy of beings. They'll switch the ends of created things. And they'll cause the biggest revolution in metaphysics, even in that part that deals with speculative knowledge. As a result, if men will want to know or discuss anything sanely, they'll find they're a completely different thing from what they've been up to now or from what they've ever imagined being.

Sun: My son, these things don't make me the least bit afraid. I have about as much respect for metaphysics as I have for physics and alchemy and necromancy. Men will just have to be content being what they are. And if they don't like that, let them go on rationalizing to their ruin, arguing in the face of unarguable evidence. Nothing's to stop them. This way they can go on being whatever they choose to be—barons or dukes or emperors or anything else. This way they'll be consoled, and their judgments won't stir up any ill feelings on Earth toward me.

Copernicus: All right, let's forget about men and the Earth. My Illustrious Lord, consider what's bound to happen to the other planets. Once they see Earth doing things the way they do, becoming one of them, they won't want to stay as plain and simple and unadorned, and as deserted and woeful as they've been up to now. They won't let Earth be the only one with ornaments. They'll want their own rivers and seas and mountains and plants and, among other things, animals and inhabitants. They won't want Earth to be one bit better than they are. And so there'll be another big revolution in the Universe—an endless variety of families and new people who'll be springing up everywhere like mushrooms.

Sun: Let them, as many as want to. My light and warmth will take care of them . . . with no added expense to me. They'll find enough to feed and clothe and house and entertain them, without getting into debt.

Copernicus: But if Your Illustrious Lord pursues the question a little deeper, you'll find some worse trouble. Once the stars see that you aren't sitting on a stool but a throne . . . and you have a wonderful court around you and a flock of planets, they won't want to sit around and take it easy. They'll want to rule the way you do. And in order to have rulers, you have to have subjects. And so they'll want planets like yours. Every single one of them will want his very own. And these new planets will have to be inhabited and beautified, like the Earth. I'm not even going to mention the human race. That's practically nothing, anyway, compared to the Universe. And it's going to shrink even more once they discover those thousands of other worlds beyond it, and they learn that the tiniest star-speck in the Milky Way has a world of its own. But considering solely your own interests, I'll say that up to now you've been the first—or maybe second, after Earth—in the whole Universe. You haven't had any competition. Because the stars never burned as bright as you did. But in this new scheme, you're going to have as many equals as there are stars. And so, you'd better be careful that this change of ours doesn't impair your own dignity.

Sun: Don't you remember what your Caesar said in crossing the Alps when he happened to pass a little hamlet of some poor barbarian? He said: I'd rather be first in that hamlet than second in Rome. Well, I'd rather be first in my solar system than second in the Universe. But it isn't ambition that makes me want to change the current state of things. It's the love of peace—or to put it bluntly, laziness. I don't really care much whether I have any equals or not, or if I'm in first place or last. Unlike Cicero, I care more about ease than dignity.

Copernicus: Most Illustrious, as far as I'm concerned, I'll try to get you this ease, the best way I can. But I'm afraid that even if I succeed, it won't last very long. First of all, I'm almost sure it won't be many years before you'll be forced to start turning around like a pulley on a well or a millstone, though you'll still be standing still. But then I suspect that after a little while you'll have to start running again, but not around the Earth. O well, what does this matter to you? Maybe that revolving upon yourself will make you *want* to progress. I've said enough. Despite all these difficulties and other considerations, I'll do my best to serve you. And if it doesn't work out, you'll know I simply couldn't do it—not that I lacked courage.

Sun: Good, my dear Copernicus, try.

Copernicus: There remains only one difficulty.

Sun: Out with it. What?

Copernicus: If I do this, I don't want to be burned alive—like the phoenix. After all, I can't resurrect myself from my ashes as does that bird. I want to go on seeing Your Lordship's face.

Sun: Listen, Copernius, you know that when your philosophers were scarcely born—I mean when poetry used to rule—I was a prophet. Now permit me to prophesy for the last time—in the memory of my former powers, have faith in me. I can tell you that when you're gone, maybe some of the people who approve what you're going to do will be roasted or something like that—but as far as I know, *you* won't suffer a thing for this job. If you want proof, adopt this plan: dedicate your book to the Pope. In this manner I promise you, you won't even lose your job with the Church.

JAMES WILHELM

DIALOGUE BETWEEN AN ALMANAC PEDDLER AND A PASSER-BY

[DIALOGO DI UN VENDITORE D'ALMANACCHI E DI UN PASSAGERE]

Peddler: Almanacs! New almanacs! Need any new almanacs, sir?

Passer-by: New year's almanacs?

Peddler: Right, sir!

Passer-by: Do you think the new year is going to be a good one?

Peddler: Oh absolutely, your honor!

Passer-by: As good as last year?

Peddler: Better, oh much better!

Passer-by: As good as the year before?

Peddler: Still better, your honor.

Passer-by: But what year will it be like? Wouldn't you want the new year to be like some one of the last few we've had?

Peddler: Oh no sir! I wouldn't care for that!

Passer-by: Well, how many new years have there been since you started peddling almanacs?

Peddler: It must be twenty by now, your honor.

Passer-by: Which of the twenty would you want the new one to be like?

Peddler: Me, sir? I wouldn't know.

Passer-by: You can't remember any particular year that seemed a happy one for you?

Peddler: Fact is, I can't, your honor.

Passer-by: Still, life's a beautiful thing, don't you think?

Peddler: Sure! Everybody knows that.

Passer-by: Wouldn't you like to live your last twenty years over again or even the whole of your past life from the day you were born?

Peddler: Oh sir, I wish to God I could!

Passer-by: Even if you were to go through it all again, with all the fun and all the heartaches you've had?

Peddler: Well no; that I wouldn't want.

Passer-by: What other life would you want then? The one I've had? The king's? Whose? Don't you imagine that I—or the king—or anybody else would say what you've said, that if anyone had a chance to live his life over again he'd turn it down?

Peddler: I guess you're right; I believe that.

Passer-by: And you wouldn't live yours over again either— that is, unless you could change it?

Peddler: No, your honor, I wouldn't do that again.

Passer-by: Then what sort of a life would you like to have?

Peddler: I'd take one as it came, as God sent it, with no conditions attached.

Passer-by: A life of chance, then, without knowing what's to come, just as you don't know now what this new year carries in store for us.

Peddler: Exactly.

Passer-by: That's the kind I'd like too, and so would everybody. But this means that, up to the present, chance has treated us all badly. It's clear everyone thinks the troubles he's had outweigh the good things that came his way, since no one's willing to be born again if he's to have the same life with all its good and bad. The life we think so beautiful is not the one that's known. It's the life that's not known—not the past life, but the future. However, with the new year things will go better for us—for you and me and everybody else, and we'll start being happy. Isn't it so?

Peddler: Let's hope so, sir.

Passer-by: Well, then, show me the prettiest almanac you have.

Peddler: Here's one, your honor; this one's thirty cents.

Passer-by: And here's thirty cents for you.

Peddler: Thanks, your honor, thanks! Goodby. Almanacs! New almanacs! New calendars!

DANIEL J. DONNO

III

Pensieri

I

For a long time I refused to believe the things I shall say below, for my nature was remote from them (and the mind tends to judge others by itself) and my inclination was never to hate men but to love them. But at last experience, as if by brute force, convinced me, and I am sure that those readers who have had many dealings with mankind will confess that what I am about to say is true. Others will say I exaggerate, until experience—if they ever have direct experience of human society—sets all this before their eyes.

I say that the world is a league of scoundrels against the men of good will, and of the petty against the generous. When two or more scoundrels meet for the first time, they easily recognize one another for what they are, as if by signs, and they are in agreement at once. Or if their interests do not permit agreement, at least they feel an attraction toward one another and have great mutual respect. If one scoundrel has dealings and contracts with another, it frequently happens that he behaves honestly and does not cheat him, but if he is dealing with honorable people, it is impossible for him to keep from breaking faith and trying to ruin them, whenever he finds it convenient. He does this even when they are men of spirit, capable of vengeance, for he hopes—as he almost always succeeds in doing—to defeat their bravery with his fraud. Many times I have seen the most timid men, finding themselves between a still more timid scoundrel and a courageous respectable man, embrace the cause of the scoundrel out of fear. In fact, this happens almost always when ordinary people are in such situations, because the ways of the courageous man of good will are known and few, but those of the rogue are mysterious and infinitely varied. Now as everyone knows, mystery is more frightening than what is known, and one may easily protect himself from a generous man's revenge and be saved by his own fear and meanness; but no fear or meanness is enough to save one from secret persecutions, slanders, or even from the open assault of base enemies. Generally speaking, in daily life true courage is little feared; for being unaccompanied by any imposture, it lacks that apparatus that makes things frightful, and so it is often not believed. And scoundrels are feared as if they were courageous because their imposture is so valiant that often it passes for bravery.

Poor scoundrels are rare, for apart from any other consideration, if a good man falls on hard times, nobody helps him and many rejoice; but if a rogue becomes poor, the whole city bestirs itself to aid him. The reason is easily understood; it is this: We are naturally touched by the misfortunes of a companion, a colleague, because they seem to menace us as well, and we give willingly all the assistance we can, for too great neglect will seem to agree that, when the time came, the same should be done to us. Now the scoundrels of the world, who are the greatest in number and in means, believe that all other scoundrels, even those they do not know by sight, are their companions and colleagues, and in times of stress feel bound to succour them through that kind of league that exists among them, as I have said. It seems scandalous to them that a rogue should be seen in distress, because though the world calls poverty honorable and virtuous, in such cases it is more likely called scourge, a thing that brings opprobrium and harm to them all. Therefore they work so effectively to remove this scandal that, except for the completely obscure, one sees few examples of rogues fallen on hard times who cannot patch up their affairs in a suitable fashion.

On the other hand, the good and the magnanimous, different from the general run, are considered by them creatures of some other species and thus not only impossible as companions but also unfit sharers of any social rights and—as we can see anywhere—persecuted more or less seriously depending on how outstanding are the baseness and the maleficence of the time and the people where the good men happen to live. For as Nature tends always to purge the bodies of animals of those principles and humors which are not in accord with the body's composition, so in aggregations of many men that same Nature insists that whoever differs from the majority, especially if that difference is contrary, must be sought out to be destroyed or driven off. And it also is customary to hate intensely the good and the generous because ordinarily they are sincere and call things by their right names. A fault not pardoned by the human race, which hates not so much the evildoer, or the evil itself, as the man who gives it a name. So that many times, while the evil-doer becomes rich, honored, and powerful, the man who names him is dragged to the scaffold, for men are ready to suffer anything from others or from heaven itself, provided that, when it comes to words, they are untouched.

X

The greater part of the people we assign to educate our sons we know for certain are not educated. Yet we do not doubt that they can give what they have not received, a thing which cannot be otherwise acquired.

XI

There are some centuries which—apart from everything else —in the arts and other disciplines presume to remake everything because they know how to make nothing.

XV

Chilon, numbered among the seven sages of Greece, ordered that the man strong in body should be gentle in behavior, as he said, to inspire in others more respect than fear. There cannot be an excess of affability, gentle manners, or even humility in those people who in beauty or genius or some other desirable quality are superior to the general run. Because the fault for which they must seek pardon is too grave, the enemy they must placate too proud and difficult; the fault is their own superiority, the enemy is envy. The ancients, when they were great and prosperous, sought to appease envy even among the Gods, expiating with acts of humility and voluntary penances that almost inexpiable sin of happiness and excellence.

XXI

In speaking, we feel no real or lasting pleasure unless we are allowed to speak of ourselves, of the matters that occupy us, or of things that are in some way ours. Every other subject in brief time grows boring, and what is pleasant to us is mortally tedious to whoever must listen. We do not acquire a reputation for amiability except through suffering, because the amiable man, in conversation, is the one who gratifies the egotism of others, who listens much and is often silent, a most boring state for him; then he allows others talk of themselves and their affairs as much as they wish; in fact, he leads them towards these subjects, and speaks of them himself, until when they take leave of one another, they find that the speakers are highly pleased with themselves, and he is highly bored with them. Because, in short, if the best company is that which we leave feeling most satisfied with ourselves, it follows that it is the company we leave most bored. The conclusion is that in conversation and other colloquy whose only aim is to pass the time in speech, almost inevitably one man's pleasure is the other man's boredom, nor can one hope to do other than to be bored or to be boring, and we are lucky indeed when we can do both equally.

XXXII

As he progresses in practical knowledge of life, man loses every day a little of that severity for which young men, always seeking perfection and expecting to find it, measuring everything by their idea of it, are so loath to pardon faults, to grant respect to slight or defective achievements, to the virtues of small moment, which they find in men.

Later when they see that everything is imperfect and are convinced that there is nothing better in the world than that slight good that they scorn, that almost nothing or no one is truly to be esteemed, then little by little, their measure changes, and comparing what comes before them not to the perfect but to the true, they grow accustomed to forgive more freely and to respect every mediocre achievement, every shade of merit, every slight talent that they find; until at last they judge praiseworthy many things and people that would at first have seemed hardly bearable.

The situation progresses until, where at first they were almost unable to feel respect, now they are virtually incapable of scorn, especially when they are richer in intelligence. For in fact, to be very scornful and incapable of contentment, when early youth is past, is not a good sign, for such people, either through lack of intelligence or slight experience, must not have come to know the world, or else they are among those fools who despise others because they hold themselves in such high esteem. And at last, it seems improbable, but it is true and is only a sign of the extreme baseness of human affairs to say that the custom of the world teaches us more to appreciate than to depreciate.

LIV

Let it be a general axiom that, except for the brevity of time, man never leaves off, in spite of any certainty and evidence to the contrary, believing, perhaps secretly, in the truth of those things where belief is necessary to the peace of his spirit and, so to speak, to enable him to live. The old man, especially if he is in society, in the privacy of his thoughts, though he may protest the oposite, never stops believing that, through some singular exception of the universal rule, he can in some unknown and inexplicable way still make an impression on women; because his condition would be too wretched if he were convinced of his exclusion forever from that boon where civilized man, now in one way and now in another, protesting more or less, comes to set the usefulness of his life.

The licentious woman, though she may see all day long a thousand signs of the public's opinion of her, believes constantly that she is considered chaste by most people, and that only a small number of her confidants, old and new (I say small in respect to the general public) know her true nature, which they keep hidden from the world and from one another.

The man of base behavior, both because of his own baseness and his slight daring, solicitous of others' opinion, believes that his actions are interpreted in the best light and their true motives are not misunderstood.

Similarly in material things, Buffon observes that the sick man at point of death does not give real credence to his doctors or to his friends but only to his own intimate hope, which promises him an escape from his present danger.

I omit the stupendous credulity of husbands about their wives, the subject of novels, scenes, jokes, and eternal laughter in those nations where matrimony is irrevocable.

And discoursing thus, there is nothing in the world so false or so absurd that it is not believed true by the most sensible men, whenever the spirit cannot accommodate itself to the opposite and give itself peace. I will not leave out the fact that the old are less disposed than the young to resist believing what suits them best and to embrace those beliefs that seem offensive; for the young have more courage to raise their eyes to evil, and more aptitude either to bear their knowledge or to perish from it.

LXIV

The artisan or scientist or the follower of whatever discipline who has the habit of comparing himself not with other followers but with the discipline itself will have a lower opinion of himself, the more excellent he is; for knowing better the profundity of his subject, the more inferior he will find himself in contrast. So almost all great men are modest, because they continually confront themselves, not with other men, but with that idea of perfection that they have in their spirit, an idea far clearer and greater than that of the crowd; and they think how far they are from attaining it. Whereas the vulgar easily, and perhaps rightly at times, believe not only that they have attained, but even surpassed the idea of perfection that is cramped in their spirits.

LXXIX

A young man never acquires the art of living nor has, one might say, any success in life or any pleasure in that art so long as his desires continue to be strong. The colder he grows, the more adept he becomes in dealing with men and with himself. Nature, with her customary beneficence, has ordained that man shall not learn how to live until the reasons for living are stolen from him, that he shall find no enjoyment until he has become incapable of vivid pleasure. Many enter the state I speak of while they are still very young, and they frequently turn out well because their desire is slight, since in their spirits their age of virility is taken over by the competition of intelligence and experience. Others never in their lives reach the state in question; they are those in whom the strength of feeling is so great at the beginning that in the course of years it does not fail; they are the ones who more than any others would enjoy life, if Nature had intended life to be enjoyed. But on the contrary, they are utterly unhappy and like children to the end in the manner of the world which they cannot comprehend.

LXXXI

It happens in conversation as with writers, many of whom please us enormously at the beginning, when we find their ideas fresh and original, but bore us as we read on to discover that one part of their writings imitates another. And so in conversation new people are often welcome and highly valued for their manner and speech; and the same people grow tiresome with acquaintance and decline in one's esteem; for men necessarily, some more and some less, when they do not imitate others, are imitators of themselves. Therefore travelers, especially if they are men of some intelligence and possess the art of conversation, easily leave behind them in the places they visit an opinion of themselves that is far superior to the truth, given the opportunity they have to conceal what is the usual defect of wit, that is poverty. For that amount that they put forth in one or a few meetings, speaking principally of the subjects they know best, whereon they are invited to speak, even without artifice, by the courtesy or curiosity of the others, what they say is believed to be not their entire store of information but only a tiny part of it and, so to speak, their daily pocket-money, not the whole sum or the greater part of their wealth. And this belief holds firm through lack of opportunity to destroy it. For the same reason, on the other hand, travelers are easily inclined to err, judging too highly the capacity of people whom they come across in their travels.

LXXXIII

If those few truly worthy men who seek glory were to know, one by one, the people who make up that public by which the seeker of glory strives with a thousand hardships to be esteemed, it is believable that they would grow cold in their endeavor or perhaps abandon it altogether. But our mind cannot escape from the power that the number of men has over the imagination, and infinitely often it is clear that we appreciate, even respect—not a multitude—but ten people gathered in a room, each of whom, taken by himself, we consider of no account.

LXXXVI

The surest way of concealing from others the boundaries of one's own knowledge is not to overstep them.

LXXXIX

Whoever communicates little with men is rarely a misanthrope. True misanthropes are not found in solitude, but in the world: because it is practical experience of the world and not philosophy that makes men hate. And if such a man retires from society, in his retirement he loses his misanthropy.

CIV

The education received, especially in Italy, by those who are educated (who, to tell the truth, are not many) is a formal betrayal ordered by weakness against strength, by age against youth. The old come and say to the young: "Beware the pleasures that belong to your age, since they are all perilous and contrary to good behavior and since we who enjoyed them as much as we could would enjoy them still if we could, but we are no longer able because of our years. Take no heed to live today, but be obedient, suffer, and slave as much as you know how to, to live later when there will be no more time." Wisdom and Honesty want the young man to abstain so far as he can from using his youth except to outstrip others in labor. "Of your future and of every other important thing leave matters to us and we will direct everything in your best interest. Each of us did the exact opposite of these things at your age and would do so again if we could be rejuvenated, but you mark our words, and not our past deeds or our intentions. And doing so, believe that we know and are experts in human affairs, and you will be happy." I know not what deceit and fraud may be if not to promise happiness to the inexperienced in such terms.

The interest of common tranquillity, domestic and public, is contrary to the pleasures and the endeavors of the young; and therefore even good education, or so called, consists largely in deceiving the pupils so that they may postpone their own comfort for the sake of others. But aside from this, the old tend naturally to destroy, as far as they can, and to cancel youth from human life, since the sight of it is abhorrent to them. In all times age was foresworn against youth, for in all times it has been characteristic of man to condemn and persecute in others those blessings that he would most desire for himself. But still it is no less remarkable that among educators who, if ever anyone in the world did, profess to seek their neighbor's welfare, one finds so many who seek to deprive their pupils of the greatest blessing of their lives, that is youth. It is even more remarkable that no mother or father, no instructor, ever felt his conscience hurt at giving his children an education inspired by such an evil principle. Which would be still more amazing if, for a long time now, for other reasons, the abolition of youth had not been believed to be a meritorious undertaking.

The fruit of such malevolent culture, which intends to benefit the cultivator by ruining the plant, is either that the students have lived like old men in the age of their flowering, become ridiculous and unhappy in old age, desiring to live like boys; or rather, as more often happens, Nature conquers, and the young, living like youths in spite of their education, become rebellious toward their teachers, who if they had favored the use and enjoyment of their youthful gifts could have regulated them through the trust of their students, which they would not have lost.

WILLIAM FENSE WEAVER

A GIACOMO LEOPARDI CHRONOLOGY

1798   Giacomo Leopardi is born at Recanati on June 29.

1811–12   Completes the translation of Horace's *Ars Poetica*, and prepares a tragedy, *Pompeo in Egitto.*

1813   Compiles a *History of Astronomy (Storia dell'astronomia).*

1815   *Saggio sopra gli errori popolari degli antichi* (Essay on the Popular Errors of the Ancients).

1816   Translates from Homer and Virgil. Undergoes what he will later call his "literary conversion." Writes his first original poem, "Appressamento della morte."

1817   Begins writing his diary-notebook, *Zibaldone.* Falls in love with a cousin, Gertrude Cassi-Lazzari, whose visit inspires his composition "Primo amore" ("First Love").

1818   *Discorso di un italiano intorno alla poesia romantica.* Following the visit of Pietro Giordani, L. writes "All'Italia" and "Sopra il monumento di Dante." Both poems appear in print in Florence the following year.

1819   Writes "L'infinito" and "Alla Luna." Beginning of his "philosophic conversion."

1820   "La sera del dí di festa."

1821   Writes several additional poems, among which are "Bruto minore," "Il sogno" and "La vita solitaria."

1822   "Alla primavera," "Ultimo canto di Saffo." Departure for Rome, where he is to stay with an uncle, Carlo Antici.

1823   Completes several philological studies. In May he returns to Recanati. There he composes "Alla sua donna."

1824   Writes the first twenty *Operette morali.*

1825   Travels to Bologna and Milan, following the instructions of a publisher, Antonio Fortunato Stella.

1825–26   His first *Idilly* (Idyls) are brought out in Milan. Works on a Petrarch edition with commentary. Lives for several months in Bologna, where he composes "Al conte Carlo Pepoli." Falls in love with the Countess Teresa Carniani Malvezzi. Collects his poems in a volume which he publishes with the title *Versi.*

1826–27   *Crestomazia italiana,* a two-volume anthology of Italian prose and poetry. In Bologna he meets for the first time Antonio Ranieri.

1827   His first edition of *Operette morali* is published in Milan.

1827–28   Resides in Pisa, and finishes writing "Il Risorgimento" and "A Silvia."

1828–29   Returns to Recanati in November, 1828. There he writes "Le ricordanze," "La quiete dopo la tempesta," and "Il sabato del villaggio."

1829–30   "Canto notturno di un pastore errante dell'Asia." He also presumably finishes "Il passero solitario." In April leaves Recanati for the last time and travels to Florence.

1830–31   Resides in Florence, thanks to a grant awarded by Pietro Colletta, a general and a historian, on behalf of a number of friends of the poet. Falls in love with Fanny Targioni-Tozzetti, and begins writing the *Paralipomeni della Batracomiomachia.* His first edition of the *Canti* appears in Florence in 1831.

1831   Together with his friend and companion Antonio Ranieri, Leopardi leaves Florence.

1832   Spends the year partly in Rome and in Florence. Completes two other *operette morali,* "Dialogo di un venditore d'almanacchi e di un passeggere," and "Dialogo di Tristano e di un amico." On December 4, 1832, writes the last page of the *Zibaldone.*

1833   Leaves Florence, and goes to Naples. .

1834–35   Writes "Aspasia." The second edition of the *Operette morali* is published in Florence. Composes two canzoni, "Sopra un bassorilievo antico sepolcrale," and "Sopra il ritratto di una bella donna scolpito nel monumento spolcrale della medesima."

1835   Composes "Palinodia al marchese Gino Capponi." The publisher Sarita of Naples begins the publication of Leopardi's *Opere.* Two volumes are brought out: *Canti,* and the *Operette morali* (but an incomplete edition).

1836–37   At Torre del Greco, Leopardi writes "La ginestra o il fiore del deserto," and "Il tramonto della luna."

1837   Leopardi dies on June 14, in Ranieri house.

A BIBLIOGRAPHICAL NOTE

BY SERGIO PACIFICI

The list of critical works on Giacomo Leopardi is, as can be imagined, vast. The English-speaking reader might begin by consulting Iris Origo's sensitive biography of the poet, *Leopardi: a Study in Solitude* (London: Hamish Hamilton, 1953), and John H. Whitfield's penetrating *Giacomo Leopardi* (Oxford: Basil Blackwell, 1954). G. Singh has recently produced an absorbing study of *Leopardi and the Theory of Poetry* (Lexington: University of Kentucky Press, 1964). In Italian, the most illuminating studies of the poet are: Francesco De Sanctis, *Leopardi* (Milan: Feltrinelli, 1958); R. Giani, *L'estetica nei "Pensieri" di G. L.* (Turin: Chiantore, 1955); A. Graf, *Foscolo, Manzoni e Leopardi* (Turin: Chiantore, 1955); Benedetto Croce, *Poesia e non Poesia* (Bari: Laterza, 1922) and *Poesia antica e moderna* (Bari: Laterza, 1941); Giovanni Gentile, *Poesia filosofia di G. L.* (Florence: Sansoni, 1960); A. Zottoli, *Storia di un'anima* (Bari: Laterza, 1947); Piero Bigongiari, *L'elaborazione della lirica leopardiana* (Florence: LeMonnier, 1948); Giovanni Ferretti, *Vita di G. L.* (Bologna: Zanichelli, 1945); Giuseppe de Robertis, *Saggio sul L.* (Florence: Vallecchi, 1959).

The reader wishing to continue his studies of Leopardi may consult the bibliographical work of G. Mazzatinti, M. Menghini, Giulio Natali and G. Musmarra in *Bibliografia leopardiana* (Florence: Olschki, 1931–1953), 3 vols.

INDEX OF ITALIAN TITLES

INDEX OF TRANSLATORS